SURPRISE PACKAGE

DUNCAN GREENWOOD
and
DEREK PARKES

SAMUEL  FRENCH

LONDON
NEW YORK TORONTO SYDNEY HOLLYWOOD

Copyright © 1975 by Duncan Greenwood and Michael Derek Parkes
All Rights Reserved

SURPRISE PACKAGE is fully protected under the copyright laws of the British Commonwealth, including Canada, the United States of America, and all other countries of the Copyright Union. All rights, including professional and amateur stage productions, recitation, lecturing, public reading, motion picture, radio broadcasting, television and the rights of translation into foreign languages are strictly reserved.

ISBN 978-0-573-01585-4

www.samuelfrench.co.uk
www.samuelfrench.com

FOR AMATEUR PRODUCTION ENQUIRIES

UNITED KINGDOM AND WORLD
EXCLUDING NORTH AMERICA
plays@samuelfrench.co.uk
020 7255 4302/01

Each title is subject to availability from Samuel French, depending upon country of performance.

CAUTION: Professional and amateur producers are hereby warned that *SURPRISE PACKAGE* is subject to a licensing fee. Publication of this play does not imply availability for performance. Both amateurs and professionals considering a production are strongly advised to apply to the appropriate agent before starting rehearsals, advertising, or booking a theatre. A licensing fee must be paid whether the title is presented for charity or gain and whether or not admission is charged.

The Professional Repertory Rights in this play are controlled by Samuel French Ltd, 24-32 Stephenson Way, London NW1 2HD.

No one shall make any changes in this title for the purpose of production. No part of this book may be reproduced, stored in a retrieval system, or transmitted in any form, by any means, now known or yet to be invented, including mechanical, electronic, photocopying, recording, videotaping, or otherwise, without the prior written permission of the publisher. No one shall upload this title, or part of this title, to any social media websites.

The right of Duncan Greenwood and Michael Derek Parkes to be identified as author(s) of this work has been asserted in accordance with Section 77 of the Copyright, Designs and Patents Act 1988.

TO
THE TITHE FARM PLAYERS
RAYNERS LANE
who bravely attempted
the first production

NOTE FOR PRODUCERS

Although not essential, the use of a rostrum as indicated on the plan will simplify problems of grouping, particularly in those scenes where all the cast are on stage at the same time. It will also enable Mildred, in Act I, Scene 2, to position herself on a level above Fritz and facilitate the pouring of the champagne into his snorkel.

The furniture on set should be of the "garden" type. White-painted wooden or metal chairs and tables are effective. The bench should have a back and arms—a white-painted park bench would be suitable. The wicker easy chair should have a high back to enable Alfred to hide behind it in Act II, Scene 1.

Some of the essential properties may be difficult to obtain and the following suggestions may prove to be helpful. Harmless but effective sea urchins can be made from potatoes impaled with the bristles from a stiff broom. A bottle which breaks realistically can be manufactured from a plastic cordial bottle. Prepare it by cutting in half leaving jagged edges. Rejoin and stick together using two small pieces of sellotape. The whole bottle should then be covered with a thin film of polyfilla and painted an appropriate colour.

CHARACTERS

Juanito, the proprietor of the "Pension Maria"
Fritz Grotz, a German tourist
Alfred Tinsley, an English tourist
Ron Tinsley, his son
Nora Tinsley, Alfred's wife
Grandma Hardcastle, his mother-in-law
Elsie Hardcastle, his sister-in-law
Mildred Armitage, an English tourist. A widow
Gloria Armitage, her daughter
Rosita, a maid at "Pension Maria"
Greta, a tourist

The action takes place on the covered patio of the "Pension Maria" in Formentera, the smallest of the Balleric Islands in the Mediterranean.

ACT I
    Scene 1   A sunny day in mid-August
    Scene 2   The following morning

ACT II
    Scene 1   The following lunch-time
    Scene 2   Early next morning

Time – the present

ACT I*

SCENE 1

The patio of the "Pension Maria" in Formentera, the smallest of the Balleric Islands in the Mediterranean. A brilliant sunny day in mid-August in the 1970's

The patio has been roofed over but is open on one side apart from a low parapet wall in which there is an opening leading down steps, off, to the beach and road. Shrubs and tall flowering plants are growing behind the wall, and beyond can be seen the sea. On the opposite side is a bar above which is an arched opening leading to the kitchen and other parts of the hotel. In the back wall is another arched opening leading to the dining-room and other parts of the hotel. Close beside this arch is a high-backed wicker chair. There are two high stools at the bar, a bench and coffee-table, and another small table. On the wall above the kitchen entrance is a letter-rack of a type which enables letters addressed to guests to be displayed and easily identified. On a small shelf below the same entrance is a telephone with a long lead, and behind the bar are shelves on which a variety of bottles is displayed

When the Curtain rises, the proprietor of the Pension, Juanito Gonzales, is behind the bar polishing glasses. After a few seconds Fritz Grotz, a newly arrived guest, enters from the kitchen arch. He looks round for someone in authority, sees Juanito, and moves to the bar to speak to him. He is somewhat irritated

Fritz Ah! Señor!
Juanito Buenas tardes, Herr Grotz. En que puedo servirle?
Fritz Es gibt kein wasser!
Juanito Que hay, señor?
Fritz Noch einmal sag'ich Ihnen. Es gibt kein wasser! Comprendo?
Juanito Lo siento, señor. No comprendo. No hablo aleman.
Fritz Gott in Himmel! (*Slowly*) Habla usted ingles?
Juanito A little, señor.
Fritz Then achtung, please!
Juanito I am all attention, señor. You wish for something?
Fritz I vish for my vater. I haff none.
Juanito It is the climate, señor. Here you must drink plenty.
Fritz The vater in the pipes. I turn on the tap and vot 'appens?
Juanito Water, señor?
Fritz No. Air. Psst! (*He hisses loudly*)
Juanito reacts

---

*N.B. Paragraph 3 on page ii of this Acting Edition regarding photocopying and video-recording should be carefully read.

Juanito (*with dignity*) There is no psst in the pipes of Pension Maria, señor!
Fritz I tell you there is nothing but psst in the pipes of Pension Maria! An hour since I turn on the tap—psst!—Half an hour since—psst!—Ten minutes—psst! psst! psst! Vot haff you to say to that?
Juanito I am sorry you have found only wind in the pipes, señor.
Fritz Psst—and vind!
Juanito I am sorry whatever it was, señor.
Fritz But I vish to vash.
Juanito There is always the sea, señor.
Fritz (*horrified*) Vash in the sea?
Juanito We have done it for centuries, señor.
Fritz Gott! In the sea!
Juanito No, señor. Gott is in heaven. But do not distress yourself. There will be water. I promise you.
Fritz Ven?
Juanito Tonight, señor. When the well has filled up again then the pump will work.
Fritz But I vish for my bath now.
Juanito You must be patient, señor. Like the English. They wait always for Friday nights.
Fritz Tonight is Friday.
Juanito And the water will be there, señor. I promise you.

The sound of an ancient taxi drawing up outside is heard

Fritz But tonight is no good. I vish for my bath now!
Juanito Please, señor, please. The English. They arrive. Excuse me.

Juanito exits down the steps

Fritz follows and looks over the parapet wall. Voices are heard off, and the slamming of taxi doors

Juanito enters up the steps carrying two battered suitcases. He is followed by Ron and Alfred, each carrying a suitcase

Welcome, señors, welcome to Pension Maria. Place your baggage down and I will arrange to take it to your rooms.
Alfred Er—thanks. (*Seeing Fritz*) How do you do?
Fritz (*solemnly*) There is no vater here.
Alfred Well that'll make a change from England. We've had plenty there this summer. (*To Juanito*) What about the rest of the baggage?
Juanito Leave it to me, señor.
Alfred But I've got to pay the taxi...
Juanito There is no charge, señor.
Alfred No charge?
Juanito It is all covered. Sunkissed Tours take care of everything. Also the taxi driver is my cousin. Excuse please.

Act I, Scene 1 3

Juanito exits down the steps

Alfred Well, that's a good start. No taxi fares.
Fritz And no vater.
Nora (*off*) Alfred!
Alfred Oh hell. (*Shouting*) Hello?
Nora (*off*) What do you want to go rushing off like that for?
Alfred (*moving to the parapet wall*) I'm seeing to the luggage.
Nora (*off*) Well come back and help Mother out of the taxi!
Alfred Here we go. I should have helped her under it long ago. (*To Ron*) Go and give Grandma a hand, Ron.
Ron All right, Dad.

Ron exits down the steps

Alfred Have you brought your mother-in-law with you?
Fritz Please?
Alfred Your mother-in-law. Your wife's mother.
Fritz No. I am here with only myself.
Alfred I see. Just the two of you.
Fritz Please?
Alfred Never mind. You're lucky to have no mother-in-law.
Fritz And no vater.

Nora appears at the parapet

Nora A fine thing to do, I must say. Leaving me stuck there to cope with Mother. You know what it's like getting her up once she's got down.
Alfred It wasn't my idea to bring her.
Nora Never mind who's idea it was. Now she's here she's got to be looked after.
Alfred And that means me, I suppose.
Nora It means all of us.
Alfred Well I've done all the looking after her so far. It was me who got her out of the taxi at Luton and nearly ruptured myself shoving her up them steps on to the plane.
Nora Well, you weren't so clever getting her off at Ibiza. If I hadn't been there she'd have fallen down them.
Alfred You mean if *I* hadn't been there. It was me she fell on.
Nora You were supposed to be supporting her.
Alfred Can I help it if she lost her shoe?
Nora No but you could have controlled your language. I don't know what those people thought behind us. I'm glad they weren't going further than Ibiza. If they'd come here I'd never have been able to look them in the face. Phew! It's hot! I could do with a drink.
Fritz There is no vater.
Alfred You don't think we've come here to drink water, do you?
Nora Speak for yourself, Alfred. And introduce me to the gentleman.

Alfred How can I? I don't even know him myself.
Fritz (*bowing and clicking his heels*) Gnädige Frau! Fritz Grotz! At your service!
Nora (*putting on a posh voice*) Charmed I'm sure. We are the Tinsley family. This is my husband Alfred. And I'm—er—Nora.
Fritz And I am German and have just arrived also.
Nora It seems a lovely place here, I must say. A real retreat from the cares of civilization. No traffic, no rain, no crowds . . .
Fritz And no vater.
Alfred Oh, for crying out bloody loud. Who the hell wants water?
Nora Alfred, please!
Fritz I haff been crying out bloody loud but the proprietor vill not listen.
Alfred Perhaps he's deaf.
Fritz That is not so. I tell him 'e has vind in his pipes. And vot does 'e do?
Alfred Take an Alka-seltzer?
Fritz No. All 'e does is apologize.
Alfred I should think so too.
Nora At least he sounds very polite.
Fritz Who vants politeness ven the vind is causing me so much trouble?
Alfred I thought you said it was troubling him.
Fritz No. 'e has vind till tonight, then 'e makes vater.

Nora looks in horror at Alfred

Nora (*to Alfred, ignoring Fritz*) I think I should like to go to my room, Alfred.
Alfred We've got to wait for the señor . . .
Nora I'd like to go now.
Alfred But we don't know where it is.
Fritz Ven you reach your room you vill find I am right.
Nora (*icily*) Really?
Fritz Until 'e makes vater you vill not be able to vash.
Nora Good heavens!
Fritz It is true. 'E tell me 'imself.
Nora Alfred, please. I can't listen to any more of this.
Alfred Grandma said we should have gone to Blackpool.
Nora Never mind about Blackpool. I want to go to my room.

Juanito enters from the parapet carrying two more suitcases

Alfred Ah, here's the señor . . .
Juanito The rest of your family are coming. Please sit for a moment and I will get you a drink.
Alfred My wife wishes to go to her room. If you could just show us where it is . . .
Juanito A momento, señor, please. (*He dives behind the bar*) When your family is here we will discuss the accommodation. What would you like? Something long to quench the thirst, eh?

Act I, Scene 1 5

Nora I don't want anything to drink.
Alfred But you said you were thirsty a few moments ago.
Nora I just want to go to my room.
Juanito Ah, señora, you are tired? You wish to rest, eh? I know how you feel.
Nora You do not.
Juanito It is the heat. Here it is too much.
Nora It's nothing of the sort. If you really want to know what it is, it's him! (*She nods in the direction of Fritz*) I don't want to stay in his presence any longer.
Juanito Señora! He has insulted you?
Alfred No, no, it's nothing—nothing at all really . . .
Nora It may be nothing to you, Alfred Tinsley, but at least there are limits to what one discusses with strangers.
Alfred Aw, come off it, Nora. He was only telling us what the conditions are like here. We've heard nothing new. We were told not to drink the water on the Continent. Now we know why.
Juanito Ah, I see. Herr Grotz has been telling you all about my water trouble? Do not worry. The problem will be over tonight.
Nora So we've been informed.
Fritz I do not understand. Is it not correct to discuss vater in England?
Alfred It depends on the water. If it's yours or mine the answer's no. If it's everyone's then it's all right. See what I mean?
Fritz No.
Alfred Well, put it another way. If it's water you drink that's one thing, but if it's water you——
Nora Alfred!
Alfred But——
Nora That's enough!
Alfred I can't let it go at that. Understanding between nations is important. The Common Market'll never work if we can't even sort our bladders out.
Nora Alfred! Please!
Juanito (*appearing swiftly from behind the bar with a tray full of glasses and a carafe of water*) Let us all have a drink. (*He puts a glass before Nora*) For you, señora. (*One before Alfred*) Señor. And Herr Grotz—for you . . . with the compliments of Pension Maria. (*He passes him the carafe of water*) Till tonight, when all will be well with the well.
Fritz Danke. (*He snatches the carafe*) I vill start on my teeth.

Fritz exits through the kitchen arch

Juanito Please forgive Herr Grotz. It is always difficult the first day in new surroundings. May I now wish you a happy holiday. Ah! Here comes the rest of your family.

Grandma comes slowly up the steps assisted by Ron and Elsie

Grandma What are you trying to do, Elsie? Pull me arm out of its socket?

Elsie lets go of Grandma's arm. Grandma lurches back into Ron, who is pushing from behind

That's right! Let me fall down the steps!
Elsie I'm only trying to help.
Grandma Then get me a chair.

Elsie scuttles for a chair

Not that one! (*She indicates the wicker chair by the arch*)

Elsie changes course, but is beaten to it by Juanito, who moves the chair forward invitingly

Juanito Allow me, señora.

Grandma flops into the chair

Grandma Thank you, young man.
Juanito It is the most comfortable. May you be happy in it. (*He returns to the bar*)
Grandma I shan't be happy till I've got me corsets off.
Nora Mother!
Grandma I've not sweated like this since the day you were born, Elsie.
Elsie Ooh! What a thing to say!
Grandma I were in a lather that day and no mistake.
Elsie (*embarrassed*) Mother! Please!
Grandma You were difficult then, Elsie. And you've been difficult ever since.
Elsie Really, Mother! What a thing to say in front of strangers. I'm so embarrassed I don't know which way to look.
Grandma Try turning profile. It suits you better. What are you all drinking?
Nora Orange juice.
Juanito (*appearing from behind the bar and holding a glass out to her on a tray*) Here is one for you, señora.
Grandma I don't want that muck.
Juanito Muck? What is muck?
Grandma The stuff in that glass. Haven't you got any stout?
Juanito A stout, señora?
Grandma That's right. A bottle of Guinness or a drop of Mackeson.
Juanito I am sorry, señora...
Grandma Don't say I've been dragged half way across the world just to drink orange juice. Give that to her. (*She points to Elsie*) And now get me something else. Something long...

Juanito hands the glass to Elsie

Juanito With ice...?
Grandma And a kick!
Juanito Like a mule, señora. Allow me... (*He goes quickly behind the bar and starts to mix her a drink*)
Grandma I think that young man and me are going to get on all right.

Nora Now, Mother, remember what the doctor said when he put you on the pill.
Grandma When he what?
Nora When he gave you those air-sickness pills. He told you not to drink or drive after them.
Grandma I never heard him.
Nora Well I did. And you've already taken six on the plane.
Grandma It's a pity you didn't. You'd have saved six paper bags.
Nora We're not talking about me. We're talking about you. You know as well as I do that even under normal circumstances you've got a funny tummy.
Grandma If we're getting down to personalities, yours isn't much to write home about either.
Nora Now then...
Grandma And that goes for your legs as well.
Nora That's enough, Mother!
Grandma No, it's not. When you went paddling at Blackpool last summer they looked like lumps of blue stilton.

Elsie leans over the parapet

Nora Mother! Please!
Grandma All right. You lay off my stomach and I'll lay off your legs. (*She suddenly notices Elsie leaning over the patio wall*) And you lay off that parapet, Elsie.

Elsie nearly falls over. Ron hauls her back

Elsie Don't shout at me like that, Mother. You nearly made me fall over.
Grandma What are you hanging over that parapet for anyway?
Elsie I'm trying to pick a convolvulus. It's all up the wall.
Grandma That's where you'll have us all in a minute. What do you want a convolvulus for?
Elsie They're blue ones. If I take some pressed specimens back the fourth-form botany club'll be thrilled.
Grandma Oh for heaven's sake, Elsie! Forget you're a schoolmistress. You're here to enjoy yourself—not to kill yourself!
Elsie But I am enjoying myself—really I am.
Grandma Well, look as if you are, then. Smile!

Elsie gives a wan and sickly grin

That's better. And for the rest of the holiday I don't want to hear about the fourth-form botany club—or the Brownie pack.
Alfred That's right!
Grandma And that goes for you too. I don't want to hear a word about the machine shop, the darts team *or* your perishing tropical fish.
Alfred Thanks very much. I assume I'm allowed to open me mouth to eat now and again?
Grandma As long as you do it quietly.
Nora I think we should go to our rooms and unpack.
Grandma I haven't had me drink yet.

Juanito (*emerging from the bar with a long drink in a tall glass*) Here you are, señora! A Pension Maria Special!
Grandma Thanks young man. Or should I say "grassyarse"? (*She takes the glass*)
Juanito The pleasure is mine, señora!
Grandma Cheers! (*She takes a long drink and loses her breath. She takes a few gasping breaths in an attempt to recover it*)
Juanito Señora! Are you all right? You wish for more ice?
Grandma (*breathlessly*) No—no—I'm all right. Go and mix the other half while I'm finishing this.
Nora I don't think you should have another one yet, Mother.
Grandma Don't tell me what to do when I'm on holiday.
Nora But we've all got a lot of unpacking to do.
Grandma Speak for yourself!
Nora (*to Juanito*) Would you please show us to our rooms?
Juanito Now?
Nora Yes now. My mother and sister will take one of the double rooms, my husband and I the other and my son will have the single.
Juanito I understand.
Nora Then please lead the way.
Juanito Your glass is empty.
Nora I do not want another drink.
Juanito With the compliments of the management?
Alfred That sounds a very fair offer.
Nora Shut up, you.
Alfred But it's free.
Nora I don't care whether it's free or it isn't. We don't want another drink. We want to go to our rooms. Will you please take us to them?
Juanito I am afraid there is just one slight difficulty, señora.
Nora (*with foreboding*) Oh?
Juanito But it will not worry you I am sure.
Nora I assume you're going to tell us that you haven't got a lift.
Juanito That's right, señora. And no single room either.
Nora No what?
Juanito Two rooms, that is all. Two double rooms is all that is booked for you.
Nora But this is ridiculous! We have confirmation. (*To Alfred, sharply*) Where is it?
Alfred Where's what?
Nora The letter confirming our booking.
Alfred Oh that—yes. (*He coughs and starts to empty his pockets*) Tickets—passports—traveller's cheques—Grandma's will—oh, and a post-card from cousin Ethel. I hope you've got her address. We'll have to send her one back.
Nora Never mind about Ethel's address!
Alfred (*still turning out his pockets*) Customs form—*Tropical Fish Breeder's Gazette*—pesetas . . . (*He brings out a wad of notes and starts to count them*)

Act I, Scene 1 9

Nora Don't count them now!
Alfred (*still turning out his pockets*) Baggage receipt—luggage labels—oh dear!
Nora What's the matter now?
Alfred (*holding up a letter*) I forgot to pay the gas bill.
Nora Oh for heaven's sake, Alfred, you're looking for our booking confirmation.
Alfred That's just it.
Nora Just what?
Alfred I can't find it. I think I must have left it at home.
Nora (*exasperated*) This is a fine time to find that out!
Juanito Please, please, do not worry. I will find a solution.
Nora You'd better. Otherwise Sunkissed Tours will get a piece of my mind.
Alfred And they'll never be the same after that!
Juanito I am sure you are right, señor. Tomorrow their courier will be here. We will complain together. It is their fault, I assure you.
Nora I knew you should have booked through Cook's instead of that twopenny-ha'penny little travel agency up the High Street.
Alfred I didn't do the booking. It were Ron.
Nora Then you should have made him go to Cook's, shouldn't you?
Alfred Don't get at me. I didn't muck up the bookings.
Nora No. All you did was leave the confirmation at home.
Juanito Please! Please let me make a suggestion, señora. I will put a third bed in one of the double rooms.
Alfred That'll suit me fine.
Nora Oh it will, will it?
Alfred Yes it will. Ron and me'll share one room and you three the other.
Nora You know very well I can't stand Mother's snoring.
Grandma I don't snore.
Nora Yes you do!
Grandma (*hiccoughing*) Hic!
Nora Among other things. And Elsie grinds her teeth.
Alfred Who wouldn't with your nagging.
Grandma I'm not sleeping with our Nora. She cuts her toenails in bed.
Alfred (*under his breath*) Next time with a bit of luck it'll be her throat.
Elsie Oooh!
Nora (*icily*) I beg your pardon.
Alfred Granted.
Nora What did you say?
Alfred I said you've got to take pot luck when you're in the same boat.
Nora I'm not taking pot luck with either Mother or Elsie. I came on holiday to rest and relax. It's bad enough having to sleep with you.
Alfred I like that!
Nora Well I don't. And I haven't done for the past twenty years.
Ron Cut it out, can't you? We're on holiday—not at home.
Grandma I wish we'd gone to Blackpool.
Nora Well we didn't. So you'll just have to make the best of it.

Ron Look, as I was responsible for the whole idea of this holiday, then it's up to me to do something about it. (*To Juanito*) Señor, I don't give a damn where I sleep.
Juanito You do not mind something simple?
Ron Not a bit. If you've somewhere to sling a hammock that'll suit me fine.
Juanito I have just the place.
Ron Good.
Juanito Where there is plenty of room and my father will not mind.
Nora My son is not going to sleep with your father!
Juanito No, no, señora, my father only sleeps in the day.
Nora You mean his bed's available at night?
Juanito No, that is when my mother is in it.
Nora Really!
Juanito Please, señora, do not misunderstand. I am not suggesting your son sleeps with either my mother or my father.
Nora I should hope not!
Juanito It would not be possible. My sister shares it with my mother at night and my uncle shares it with my father in the day.
Grandma Well, at least the bed'll be warm!
Juanito Please. I explain. My uncle and father are fishermen. All night they fish. So the hut where they keep the nets is empty all night. There I will sling a hammock for your son.
Nora This is ridiculous!
Alfred And there'll naturally be a reduction in the cost of our accommodation?
Juanito But of course, señor. Come, let me show you the way.

Juanito picks up two suitcases. Alfred and Ron pick up the rest. Juanito starts to shepherd them off by the kitchen arch. Grandma makes no move to follow

Nora Come on, Mother.
Grandma Don't rush me.
Juanito Please finish your drink, señora. I will return for you in a moment.

Juanito leads the way off through the kitchen arch, followed by Nora, Alfred and Ron

Elsie starts to follow. As she reaches the arch Grandma calls after her

Grandma Where do you think you're going, Elsie?
Elsie I'm just going to—er . . .
Grandma Come here.
Elsie (*dithering back to her*) But I thought if I—er—perhaps . . .
Grandma Didn't you hear what he said? He's coming back for us in a minute.
Elsie I know he did but you see . . . (*She dithers back to the arch*)
Grandma Stop dancing about. You look as though you want to go somewhere.

Act I, Scene 1   11

Elsie As a matter of fact—I do!
Grandma A fine time to choose, I must say. But you've always been the same. Couldn't take you anywhere as a child. If it wasn't in church it was on top of a bus.
Elsie I can't help it!
Grandma Well you'll just have to wait till he comes back to show you where it is.
Elsie I wish I hadn't drunk that orange juice!

Fritz enters through the kitchen arch. He moves to the others, clicks his heels and bows

Fritz (*announcing himself gutterally*) Fritz Grotz.
Grandma Elsie, lend him your hanky!
Elsie (*sotto voce*) It's his name. He's German.
Grandma Sounds more like Flemish to me.
Elsie My name is Elsie Hardcastle and this is my mother.
Fritz A pleasure! (*Clicking his heels and bowing to Elsie*) Gnädiges Fräulein! (*Clicking his heels and bowing to Grandma*) Gnädiges Frau! You are 'ere for your 'oliday?
Grandma What do you think we're here for? Pleasure?
Elsie You must excuse Mother, Herr Grotz. She wanted to go to Blackpool.
Fritz Ah Blackpool! I come here for the sun.
Grandma And I come here for me daughters. They wouldn't go where I wanted.
Fritz But you should go vere you vant. And so should they.
Grandma Oh, I couldn't let them go off on their own. Not with all this permissiveness about.
Elsie Really, Mother . . . !
Fritz I understand. A pretty girl like your daughter vould not be safe on her own.
Grandma You think so, do you?
Fritz Ja, I do.
Grandma Then maybe I should have let her go off on her own. I might have got her off me hands. No-one looks sideways at her at home.
Elsie (*hurt*) Mother!
Fritz Sideways, I agree, she is not so good. But her front side is very pretty.
Grandma That's right. Her nose isn't so noticeable from the front.
Fritz And I haff no doubt that her backside is just as attractive.
Elsie Really!
Grandma Oh, I can't agree with you there.
Fritz Turn round!
Elsie I beg your pardon?
Fritz I said turn round.
Grandma And stop jiggling about.
Elsie I'll do nothing of the sort!

Fritz But I do not understand. All I vish to tell you is that you are attractive in all directions. Do you not vish to know that?
Elsie I—I don't know—no-one's ever said anything like that to me before.
Fritz You mean in England no man has ever noticed your charms?
Elsie Well no . . .
Fritz Particularly when they are so outstanding?
Elsie I didn't know they were that.
Grandma They're not.
Fritz But I assure you. You are a typical English rose.
Elsie Oh come, Herr Grotz. I'm no rose. Am I, Mother?
Grandma Oh, I don't know. We do have Christmas roses in England.
Fritz In Germany ve 'ave few roses, but many—er—chrysanthemums?
Grandma Big and fluffy?
Fritz Ja, that is so.
Elsie You are obviously fond of flowers, Herr Grotz.
Fritz They are a great passion of mine. Especially roses.
Elsie I think perhaps I'd better go now and . . .
Fritz Not yet, please . . .
Elsie But it's rather important, you see I have to find—er—I have to find something.
Fritz That is lost?
Elsie It's not exactly lost—it's somewhere about . . .
Fritz I vill find it for you.
Elsie I can't expect you to do that . . .
Fritz I am a good searcher.
Elsie But you're a man. You couldn't even use it if you found it—I mean . . .
Fritz But I do not vish to use it.
Elsie (*to herself*) I wish I didn't.
Fritz All I vant is to find it for you. Tell me vot I must look for.
Grandma From the way she's jiggling about I should have thought that was obvious.
Fritz (*not understanding*) Jiggling?
Elsie Oh, Mother!
Grandma She wants the loo.
Elsie Mother! How could you?

Elsie runs off through the kitchen arch in embarrassment

Grandma I hope she makes it.
Fritz Who is this Lew she is looking for?
Grandma I beg your pardon?
Fritz Her young man perhaps?
Grandma She's never had one of them in her life.
Fritz Then I do not understand.

Juanito enters through the kitchen arch

Act I, Scene 1   13

Grandma You're just in time. I've reached the bottom of me glass.
Fritz (*bowing*) Please let me have the honour . . .
Grandma I don't dance.
Fritz Of buying you another drink.
Grandma I don't mind if I do. Similar please.
Fritz Similar?
Grandma Same again. It's called a Pension Maria Special. And I can recommend it!
Fritz (*to Juanito*) Another Special for the Frau please.
Juanito (*taking her glass*) A pleasure! (*He goes behind the bar to mix the drink*)

Fritz follows and stands by the bar waiting to pay for the drink

Elsie returns and moves to Grandma. She is still obviously in distress

Fritz and Juanito do not hear the following conversation between Elsie and Grandma

Grandma What's the matter? Didn't you find it?
Elsie Yes.
Grandma Then why are you still jiggling about?
Elsie I couldn't use it.
Grandma Someone were in?
Elsie No.
Grandma Then how do you mean you couldn't use it?
Elsie It's gone!
Grandma Gone? What's gone?
Elsie The pedestal. There's nothing to sit on.
Grandma You're joking!
Elsie I'm not. There's just a hole in the floor.
Grandma What sort of a hole?
Elsie A little round one.
Grandma And nothing else?

Fritz pays for the drink

Elsie No.
Grandma I said we should have gone to Blackpool.
Elsie What shall I do?
Grandma Hang on till I sort this out.

Juanito emerges from the bar to serve the drink

Juanito Your "Special", señora. With the compliments of Herr Grotz.
Grandma (*taking the drink*) Thanks very much. (*To Fritz*) Cheers!
Juanito A pleasure, señora. (*He turns to go*)
Grandma Just a minute, young man.
Juanito Señora? You wish now to go to your room?
Grandma Not till you've answered a few questions.
Juanito I see. What are the questions?

Grandma Are you in trouble?
Juanito Trouble?
Grandma Financial trouble.
Juanito You mean—with money?
Grandma That's right. You've not had the bums in or anything like that, have you.
Juanito Bums, señora?
Grandma Bum bailiffs—debt collectors.
Juanito Oh no, nothing like that.
Grandma Then who's pinched the seat from the you-know-what?
Juanito Pinched the seat?
Grandma The thing you sit on when you go.
Juanito I'm sorry, señora, I do not understand.
Grandma Me daughter's just been and she can't because there isn't one.

Juanito looks at Fritz, baffled. Fritz shrugs. Juanito shrugs

And it's no good looking at him like that. He can't help you. I must say it's coming to something if you can't sit down when you want to go.
Juanito But you are sitting, señora.
Grandma I know I am. But it's not me that wants to go—yet. It's me daughter. She wants to spend a penny.

Fritz and Juanito look at Elsie, who is still obviously uncomfortable

Juanito What is it she wishes to buy, señora?
Grandma She doesn't want to buy anything. Can't you see? She's desperate.
Juanito (*suddenly appreciating the situation*) Ah, señora! The penny has dropped! (*To Elsie*) Please, through the door, along the corridor, the door on the right with the little lady on it.
Elsie I know. I've been and there's only a hole.
Juanito Ah! But beside the hole there are two little flat places for your feet.
Elsie (*in horror*) You don't mean . . . ?
Grandma He does.
Elsie Oh!

Elsie runs off through the kitchen arch

Juanito (*apologetically*) I am afraid that in Spain . . .
Grandma It's standing room only?
Juanito Not exactly. But it is the accepted custom here.
Grandma Maybe so. But if you want me to stay in this place you'd better do something about it—quick!
Juanito But of course, señora. Anything you suggest.
Grandma Get a deck-chair installed.
Juanito A deck-chair?
Grandma With a hole cut in the seat. And now I think you'd better take me to me room . . .

Act I, Scene 1   15

Juanito Certainly, señora.
Grandma For the inspection.
Juanito Inspection?
Grandma To make sure everything's there—including the gazzunder!

Juanito, carrying the rest of the luggage, shepherds Grandma off through the kitchen arch

As soon as he is alone, Fritz nips quickly behind the bar and helps himself to a drink

Mildred and Gloria enter from the parapet

Mildred sees Fritz behind the bar and assumes he is the barman

Mildred (*to Gloria*) I'm not going to argue, Gloria. We'll discuss that later. (*To Fritz*) Dos quantros con hielo por favor, señor.
Gloria Oh Mum, I'd rather have a beer. I'm thirsty.
Mildred Perdone usted, señor. Un quantro con hielo y una cerveza por favor.

Fritz stares at Mildred

No comprendo?
Fritz I vill if you speak English.
Mildred English? Then that's thirty quid wasted on that bloody Linguaphone course.
Fritz I apologize. But you see I am not the barman. I am a guest.
Mildred Then what are you doing behind the bar?
Fritz Juanito is not here, so I help myself.
Mildred Then while you're at it you can give me a beer and a quantro con hielo.
Fritz And a vot?
Mildred Oh, make it two beers.
Fritz Two beers it is. (*He starts to pour them out*)
Gloria I do wish we'd gone to Ibiza.
Mildred For heaven's sake stop moaning. We've only been here a couple of hours.
Gloria But there's no nightclubs or nothing. It's all sand.
Mildred We didn't come here for nightclubs.
Gloria Well, I didn't come here for sand.

Fritz emerges from the bar with the beers

Mildred (*taking one*) Ooh! That looks all right!
Gloria (*taking the other*) Thanks.
Fritz (*clicking his heels*) Now I vill introduce myself. Fritz Grotz. I too have just arrived.
Mildred I'm Mildred Armitage. And this is my daughter, Gloria.
Fritz (*clicking his heels again*) Gnädiges Fräulein!
Mildred Do you come here often, Mr Grotz?

Fritz No, I go different places each year.
Mildred Very wise. We do the same.
Gloria We do what?

Mildred deliberately treads on Gloria's toes

Ow! That was my foot!
Mildred Then keep it out of the way. As I was saying, it broadens one's outlook to travel abroad. And see how the other half live, as you might say.
Fritz Ja, that is so. Your 'usband is 'ere vith you?
Mildred No, I'm afraid not. I'm a widow.
Fritz Ah!
Mildred (*sighing*) Poor Samuel! He passed on two years ago.
Fritz I am sorry.
Gloria You needn't be. She wasn't.
Mildred Gloria! (*To Fritz*) One must try to be strong and not grieve, Mr Grotz. Life must go on.
Fritz And on.
Mildred Quite. Your family is with you?
Fritz No. I am with myself—alone.
Mildred (*showing interest*) Really? Gloria, I seem to have lost my handkerchief. Go and see if I dropped it on the way back from the beach.
Gloria I've got a clean one.
Mildred I don't want your handkerchief, dear. I want mine. Please go and have a look.
Gloria (*with bad grace*) Oh, all right.

Gloria exits by the parapet steps

Mildred Which part of Germany do you come from, Mr Grotz?
Fritz München.
Mildred Ah, the north, like me.
Fritz No, the south.
Mildred Oh, excuse me. Geography was never one of my strong subjects. I shone much more in needlework and domestic science.
Fritz Ah! I too am in science.
Mildred Not domestic science?
Fritz No, medical science.
Mildred (*impressed*) Really?
Fritz Ja.
Mildred Fancy? And I took you for the barman.

Gloria enters with the handkerchief

Gloria It was at the bottom of the steps.
Mildred Oh, thank you. (*She takes the handkerchief and mops her brow with it*) That's better. The heat here is quite exhausting. Another drink, Gloria?

Act I, Scene 1   17

Gloria No, thanks.
Mildred Not even a nice long cold orange squash?
Gloria I don't want anything.
Mildred Why don't you go for a little stroll down to the beach?
Gloria I've seen the beach, I've had a drink and I don't want anything else at the moment, thank you very much.
Mildred I'm afraid Gloria's somewhat bored, Mr Grotz. Young people do like a bit of life when they're on holiday. And from what we've seen so far it looks as though things are going to be a bit quiet for her.
Fritz New surroundings are always disappointing at first.
Mildred I quite agree.
Gloria Oh, for heaven's sake stop making excuses for me, Mum. I'm fed up. All right. So what? Let's leave it at that.
Mildred But I don't want you to be fed up.
Gloria Well I can't help it if I am, can I?
Mildred The whole idea of this holiday was to give you a change. There's no point in spending all this money if you're not going to enjoy yourself. We might just as well have stayed at home.
Gloria Let's go back home then.
Mildred Don't be ridiculous. We're booked here for a fortnight.
Fritz Do not worry, Fräulein. There vill be lots to do and many young men to keep you happy ven the new guests arrive.
Gloria I'll believe that when I see it.

Gloria exits down the steps

Mildred You must forgive Gloria, Mr Grotz. The fact is she's just had a very unhappy experience.
Fritz Ah!
Mildred She broke off her engagement a few weeks ago and hasn't got over it yet.
Fritz So she is 'ere to mend her broken heart?
Mildred That's right. It was all for the best. A most unfortunate match, it would have been.
Fritz Unfortunate?
Mildred Well, the young man wasn't too bad. But the family! You should have seen them! Common. Common as muck if you know what I mean. Not her class at all!
Fritz Vot vas wrong with them?
Mildred No breeding. No refinement. What I call a real brown-ale crowd.
Fritz Ah!
Mildred You know what I mean?
Fritz No.
Mildred Well, take the mother, for instance. If she came here she'd spend all her time bawling at her husband and moaning because she couldn't get a nice cup of tea. And her husband—he'd sit on the beach in his shirt sleeves and braces and paddle with his trousers rolled up and a handkerchief with knots in the corners of it stuck on his head.

Alfred enters through the kitchen arch, dressed exactly as described by Mildred. Nora follows him on

Alfred I tell you I don't want a cup of tea, Nora! I'm off down to the beach for a paddle. (*He sees Mildred*) Bloody hell! Look who's here!

QUICK CURTAIN

SCENE 2

The same. After breakfast the following morning

The sun is shining brilliantly. Alfred and Nora enter from the dining-room. They have just finished a late breakfast

Alfred ... And I certainly don't call that a breakfast!
Nora Don't show your ignorance. Rolls and coffee is a continental breakfast.
Alfred Well it ain't mine.
Nora When in Rome...
Alfred We're not in bloody Rome. We're in Spain.
Nora Oh, for heaven's sake don't be so blooming thick.
Alfred A fortnight of breakfasts like that and I'll be blooming thin!
Nora You've a long way to go before you starve.
Alfred Not so long as you think. I haven't eaten anything since we left the plane yesterday.
Nora You have. You had dinner last night.
Alfred A bit of melon. That's all.
Nora You should have tried the paella.
Alfred Dead scorpions in rice. That's what it looked like. Turned me right over.
Nora I hope you're not going to spend the next fortnight complaining about your stomach.
Alfred I can't help it if it's delicate. It's not recovered from the turn it got when we found that Armitage woman sitting here.
Nora That gave me quite a turn too. I always said Ron should never have booked at that tatty little travel agent up the High Street... Oh!
Alfred Oh—what?
Nora I've just had a thought.
Alfred That's a change. What about?
Nora Our Ron. I reckon he's booked us here on purpose.
Alfred Well I can't imagine he did it by accident.
Nora I mean deliberately. So he could be in the same hotel as that Gloria girl.
Alfred Why should he want to do that? He finished with her weeks ago.
Nora You mean she finished with him.
Alfred She wasn't much cop anyway. Nothing to offer apart from—er...

Act I, Scene 2   19

Nora Quite! Which reminds me, now that we're alone. I want to have a word with you about last night.
Alfred Last night? What about last night?
Nora You know.
Alfred I don't.
Nora You woke me up in the middle of the night.
Alfred And a fat lot of good it did me, didn't it?
Nora I don't know what's got into you.
Alfred Well we *are* supposed to be on holiday.
Nora That's no excuse for taking liberties.
Alfred Liberties!
Nora It was just the same last year at Blackpool.
Alfred No it wasn't. I got somewhere then.
Nora There's a time and place for everything.
Alfred And I've still got to find either.
Nora I haven't been so embarrassed for a long time. With Elsie and Mother in the next room.
Alfred Oh for heaven's sake . . .
Nora And walls as thin as paper. I could distinctly hear Mother swilling her teeth.
Alfred It didn't sound like that to me.
Nora Then you admit the walls are thin!
Alfred I don't know whether they are or they aren't. All I know is that I'm having a miserable holiday. I'd sooner be home with me guppies.
Nora You and your fish!
Alfred What's wrong with me fish?
Nora You do more for them than you do for your family.
Alfred I don't. I do exactly the same for both—I feed them!
Nora I don't know what you can see in them. They can't talk.
Alfred That's their main attraction.
Nora Well you'll have to do without them for a fortnight.
Alfred And that's not all I'll have to do without in this place.

Rosita enters with a tray and starts to collect empty glasses. She is young and attractive

No pubs, no darts, no football, no bacon and eggs, no . . . (*He suddenly catches sight of Rosita*)
Nora And no what?
Alfred (*unable to take his eyes off Rosita*) No wonder I'm feeling down in the dumps. It's a drink I need. Buenas dias, señorita!
Rosita (*smiling at him*) Buenas dias, señor.
Alfred Where did you come from? I didn't see you about yesterday.
Rosita Yesterday I have the day off, señor.
Alfred And what do you get up to on your day off then?
Rosita Get up to?
Alfred What do you do?
Rosita Swim, go for walks, sleep . . .

Alfred On your own?
Nora Alfred!
Alfred I mean do you go for walks on your own?
Rosita Not if there is anyone to go with me, señor.
Alfred I've done a bit of walking in my time with the 'Eckmondwyke 'Arriers.
Nora I think it's about time you went for a walk on the beach with me, Alfred Tinsley.
Alfred You're not getting me on the beach!
Nora And why not?
Alfred Because I don't want sunstroke, that's why not.
Nora Sunstroke? Don't be ridiculous. You went on the beach yesterday.
Alfred And I've suffered from it ever since.
Nora Suffered from what?
Alfred Sunburn.
Nora Sunburn?
Alfred On both legs. From me calves down to me ankles.
Nora If you're not going on the beach then what are you going to do?
Alfred Sit here and wait for me lunch.
Nora Then I'll stay here with you.
Alfred There's no point in you sacrificing your pleasures for me, love. If you want to go down to the beach—go. Don't let me stop you.
Nora If you think I'm going to leave you here alone with...
Alfred With what?
Nora With your—with your sunburn, and your—your stomach trouble.
Alfred Don't worry about me, love. I'll be all right.

Rosita bends down to pick something from the floor, her rear view towards Alfred

I'll just sit here quietly and enjoy the—(*he sees Rosita*)—view.
Nora View?
Alfred From the terrace. Over there. I'll be quite all right. Sitting with me feet up, sipping a nice cool beer and listening to me stomach rumbling while I'm waiting for me lunch. Señorita!
Rosita Si, señor?
Alfred A nice cold beer please.
Rosita Si, señor. Una cerveza con hielo. Pronto. (*She goes behind the bar*)
Nora And what about me?
Alfred What about you?
Nora Don't I get anything?
Alfred Certainly—next year when we go to Blackpool.
Nora Oh!

Stiff lipped, Nora marches off to the beach

Alfred (*moving to the bar*) And I'll have a bag of crisps as well,
Rosita Crisps, señor?
Alfred To put me on till dinner time.

Act I, Scene 2   21

Rosita What are crisps, señor?
Alfred You don't know?
Rosita No, señor.
Alfred They're crinkly bits of spud in a bag.
Rosita (*holding up a bag of nuts*) These, señor?
Alfred No, them's nuts. Never mind, they're better than nothing. Give us a packet.
Rosita (*handing him the nuts with his beer*) Thirty pesetas, señor. (*He pays*)

Ron enters from the kitchen arch

Ron Good morning, Dad.
Alfred Morning, Ron. Have you just got up?
Ron Yes.
Alfred Then you've missed breakfast.
Ron I'm not hungry.
Alfred Just as well. A lump of bread and a cup of coffee. That's all I got. Wasn't worth going in for. I'm having the rest of me breakfast now. (*Offering the bag of nuts to Ron*) Have some.
Ron No thanks, Dad.
Alfred A beer then?
Ron I'd rather have a coffee.
Alfred A coffee, señorita, please.
Rosita Si, señor.

Alfred starts to sniff, with a puzzled look on his face

Ron Where's mother?
Alfred (*still sniffing, and taking a quick look over the bar to see if he can locate the source of the smell that is offending him*) She's gone to the beach.
Ron What's the matter?
Alfred Hasn't it reached you?
Ron Reached me?
Alfred The Ethel M. Dell. (*He lifts his feet up one at a time and examines the soles*)
Ron The what?
Alfred The pen and ink. Lift your feet up.
Ron Why?
Alfred To see if you've trod in anything.
Ron (*displaying the underside of his soles*) All clear?
Alfred No it isn't. It's getting stronger.
Ron What's it smell like?
Alfred Stale fish. (*They both turn towards Rosita*) You don't suppose ...
Ron Suppose what?
Alfred That she's spent the last couple of hours gutting our lunch.
Rosita (*swinging round and putting the coffee on the bar*) Fifteen pesetas, please, señor.

Alfred pays. Ron stretches out his arm in front of Alfred to pick up the cup of coffee

Alfred My God, lad, it's you!
Ron Me?
Alfred It's that shirt you've got on. What have you been doing with it?
Ron (*sniffing his sleeve*) Nothing. It's the one I wore yesterday.
Alfred Then you want to change it more often.
Ron It's not me. It's the shed.
Alfred The shed?
Ron Where I slept last night. I had to put my clothes on a crab pot.
Alfred Then you'd better put them somewhere else tonight. Or sleep in them.
Ron I can't help having to sleep in the net store.
Alfred That's a matter of opinion. You booked in at this place. And deliberately, your mother thinks. Just to be with that Gloria girl.
Ron I did as a matter of fact. Any objections?
Alfred Plenty. If we'd gone to Blackpool I wouldn't be suffering from heat stroke and malnutrition.
Ron If you're all that hungry there's some packets of crisps in Mother's holdall.
Alfred Crisps?
Ron She bought them at the airport yesterday.
Alfred Then why the heck didn't you say so before?

Alfred exits quickly through the kitchen arch

Rosita Your father is miserable here?
Ron Just the opposite. He's got so much to grumble about I've never seen him so happy.

Gloria enters up the steps. She stops short on seeing Ron

Gloria Oh!
Ron Hello.
Gloria Hello.
Ron You—er—got here then?
Gloria I wouldn't be here if I hadn't, would I?
Ron No, I suppose not.
Gloria What made you come here?
Ron Well—I—thought—maybe—if . . .
Gloria If what?
Ron Well, if we saw something of each other again . . .
Gloria We might patch it up?
Ron That's right.
Gloria I suppose I should be flattered. You following me half-way across the world.
Ron Not quite as far as that.
Gloria Half-way across Europe then.

Act I, Scene 2

Ron It makes no difference mind you. Wherever you'd gone I'd have followed you. Even to the moon.
Gloria Oh Ron! (*She runs to him, throws her arms around him and kisses him*) Oh Ron, I still love you!

Rosita watches the proceedings with great interest

Ron Me too!

They kiss

Gloria Oh Ron! You don't half pong!
Ron I know. It's fish!

They kiss again

Gloria I've missed you terribly.
Ron I've missed you too!
Gloria I do wish you didn't smell so much.
Ron So do I.

They kiss again

Don't ever break it off again, will you?
Gloria It wasn't my idea.
Ron I know. It was your mum, wasn't it?
Gloria Yes.
Ron Stupid old moo!
Gloria But Ron, she is my mum.
Ron Worse luck.
Gloria She's not very happy.
Ron I wouldn't be either, if I was her.
Gloria The fact is she's lonely. Has been ever since Dad died.
Ron Where is she now?
Gloria On the beach. I've just left her.
Ron How about you and me going for a little walk in the other direction—round the olive grove?
Gloria Now?
Ron Why not?
Gloria Hang on then while I get my sun-glasses. I won't be a minute.

Gloria exits through the kitchen arch

Ron (*to Rosita*) You know something, señorita? I think I'm going to enjoy this holiday.
Rosita You appear to be enjoying it already, señor.
Ron I certainly am! Now we've patched things up everything's going to be fine! (*He swings his arm with an expansive gesture knocking his father's empty glass off the bar. It smashes on the floor*) Oh blast! I'm terribly sorry, señorita.
Rosita Do not worry, señor. I will sweep it up.
Ron No, no, it's my fault. I'll clear it up.

Ron picks up some of the pieces which have scattered towards the table. Rosita emerges from the bar with a dustpan and brush. Ron, moving beside the table, also picks up the cup of cold coffee. Rosita stands behind and slightly to one side of Ron, who is unaware she is there. He swings round with the coffee cup and pieces of broken glass in his hands with the intention of taking them to the bar

It was a stupid thing to do. I really am sorry. (*He collides with Rosita. The coffee spills down the front of her skirt*) Oh God! I didn't see you—I...

Rosita stands gazing down at her skirt. Ron quickly puts the coffee cup and broken pieces of glass on the bar, whips out his handkerchief, kneels down in front of her and starts to mop her skirt and legs. He puts one hand a little way up the inside of her skirt and mops the outside

I don't think it's gone through.
Rosita Don't worry, please.
Ron I really am sorry.

Mildred enters from the steps

Rosita It would be better if I went to my room and took my skirt off.
Ron I think you're right.
Rosita It would make things easier.
Ron I'm sorry to be so clumsy.
Rosita Don't worry.
Ron It's because I'm so excited!
Rosita I know how you feel. When two people come together again it is always exciting...
Ron You're very understanding.

Mildred coughs. Ron and Rosita turn and see her

Oh! (*He gives a feeble laugh*) I didn't know you were there, Mrs Armitage. I was just helping the señorita—she's in trouble...
Mildred Really?
Ron Yes, it was an accident...
Mildred I'm sure.
Ron It just slipped out of my hand and wet her.
Mildred Indeed!

Rosita runs off, almost colliding with Gloria, who is returning through the kitchen arch with her sun-glasses

Mildred Ah, there you are, Gloria.
Gloria I thought you were on the beach.
Mildred It's just as well I wasn't—for your sake!
Gloria Why for my sake?
Mildred You'll understand when I tell you about the disgusting scene I've just witnessed.

Ron Now look here, Mrs Armitage——
Mildred I've done all the looking I want to do, thank you very much.
Gloria What's all this about?
Ron Your mother seems to think——
Mildred It's not what I think, it's what I saw. I came up those steps about three minutes ago and caught him and that young foreign waitress girl together—right here—in broad daylight . . .
Gloria Doing what?
Mildred I can hardly bring myself to say it . . .
Gloria Oh, for heaven's sake, Mum!
Mildred They were—carrying on.
Gloria (*to Ron*) You weren't! Were you?
Ron Of course not!
Mildred Then what were you doing down on your knees? Praying?
Ron You know very well what I was doing.
Mildred You were fondling her legs!
Ron I was not.
Mildred No?
Ron No. I was patting them.
Mildred Patting or fondling, what's the difference?
Ron There's nothing wrong in what I was doing!
Mildred People have different ideas of what's right and what's wrong.
Ron I see nothing wrong in mopping her legs.
Mildred So we've got round to mopping now have we?
Ron Yes, they were wet.
Mildred And I suppose you're going to tell us you were fiddling about with her skirt because that was wet too?
Ron It was as a matter of fact.
Mildred A likely tale! She was offering to take it off when I came in.
Gloria She wasn't!
Mildred She was! And he was egging her on.
Ron I certainly was not!
Mildred Oh yes, you were. You said it would make things easier.
Ron I didn't! She said that.
Gloria Oh! I don't want to hear any more.

Gloria bursts into tears and runs off through the kitchen arch

Ron Gloria! (*To Mildred*) You did that deliberately! Just to make sure we wouldn't patch things up! Well, you know what you are, don't you?

Alfred enters from the kitchen arch with a bag of crisps

You're a malicious, scheming perverter of the truth! And if you weren't a woman I'd——
Alfred (*authoritatively*) Ron!
Ron You keep out of this, Dad!
Alfred Calm down, lad!

Ron Calm down? Do you know what she's just done?
Alfred No, but blowing your top won't help.
Ron Ach!

Ron goes off angrily down the steps

Alfred I'm sorry about Ron, Mrs Armitage. You've obviously got him into a bit of a state. What's he been up to?
Mildred I'd rather not say.
Alfred Aw, come on, get it off your chest.
Mildred Well, I came in and caught him and that Spanish waitress. (*A pause*) At it!
Alfred At what?
Mildred Don't act stupid. You know what I mean.
Alfred How far—at it?
Mildred Far enough. For ten o'clock in the morning.
Alfred (*pensively*) Oh.
Mildred Well, aren't you surprised?
Alfred I certainly am. I didn't know the lad had it in him.
Mildred You should be shocked.
Alfred Why? He is on holiday, after all.
Mildred And that makes it all right?
Alfred Look, the lad's free to please himself what he does. He's not engaged to your Gloria any longer.
Mildred And if I've anything to do with it, it'll stay that way.
Alfred Quite right. I'll drink to that.
Mildred Quite right? So Gloria isn't good enough for him now!
Alfred I didn't say that.
Mildred But you implied it.
Alfred Look, let's have a drink. (*Calling*) Juanito! Where are you? We're dying of thirst in here.
Juanito (*off*) Coming, señor.
Alfred (*to Mildred*) What'll you have?
Mildred I don't want anything.
Alfred Aw, come on. Be a devil. At least you can drink to Gloria's good luck in not getting me as a father-in-law.
Mildred (*thawing*) All right, if you insist. I'll have an orange squash.

Juanito enters through the kitchen arch

Alfred With a spot of gin in it?
Mildred A very little.
Alfred A gin-and-orange and a nice cold beer please, Juanito.
Juanito Certainly, señor.
Alfred And while we're waiting, have a crisp. (*He opens the bag of crisps*) Oh hell! Cheese and onion!
Mildred What's wrong with cheese and onion?
Alfred I don't like cheese and onion.

Mildred Perhaps he'll change them for you.
Alfred I didn't get them from him.
Mildred Oh.
Alfred Just like Nora. She bought them. And she knows I like smoky bacon.

Fritz enters from the beach, dressed in a beach-robe. He has been swimming

Oh God, here comes Himmler.
Mildred (*coldly*) I beg your pardon.
Alfred (*confidentially*) Hitler's secret weapon!
Mildred (*coldly*) I don't think that's very funny. (*Gushing to Fritz*) Ah, Herr Grotz!
Fritz Guten Morgen!
Mildred Good morning!
Alfred Good Heavens!
Mildred And what was the water like?
Fritz Vet.
Mildred But warm?
Fritz Ja. Varm and vet.
Alfred (*to himself*) That's not the only wet thing around here.
Fritz There vas many rocks in the vater. And many peoples. And many weed.
Mildred And many what?
Fritz Many weed.
Alfred That settles it. I'm not going in. Not even to paddle!
Mildred (*giving Alfred a withering look*) You mean much weed, Herr Grotz.
Fritz Ja. Plenty. All over ze place. And many little creatures with prickles on ze bottom.
Mildred On the bottom?
Fritz Of ze sea.
Mildred Oh! You mean sea urchins!
Fritz Sea urch-ins? That is how you call them? Sea urch-ins? That is good. I learn another vord. You vill teach me plenty more—ja?
Mildred (*seductively*) Plenty.
Juanito (*delivering the drinks*) Your drinks, señor. (*He gives the gin-and-orange to Mildred and the beer to Alfred*)
Alfred Ah! Thank you. (*He sits*)
Juanito Sixty pesetas, señor.
Alfred Sixty?
Juanito Fifteen for the beer, forty-five for the gin-and-orange.
Alfred (*sarcastically*) Haven't you got anything more expensive?
Juanito Only whisky, señor.

Alfred pays grudgingly

Fritz Of course I know many English vords already. There is a creature you call a grab.

Alfred A grab?
Fritz Ja. A fish vith legs and pincers.
Alfred Oh, you mean a crab.
Fritz That is right. And one vich swims standing up vich you call a yorse. A sea yorse.
Alfred A yorse? What's a yorse?
Fritz Vot's a mine? A visky and vater please.
Alfred Now wait a bit...
Fritz You are most generous.
Alfred Oh, all right. A whisky and water for Herr Grotz please.
Juanito Certainly, señor.
Fritz Now tell me some more English words.
Alfred I think you know enough already.
Fritz You are what is called in England standing a round—ja?
Alfred Ja.
Fritz That is good.
Alfred Is it? And what about in Germany?
Fritz In Germany it is different.
Alfred It would be.

Juanito places the whisky and water in front of Fritz

Fritz Danke. In Germany ve do not stand around. Ve all sit down and pay for our own.
Juanito Seventy pesetas, señor.
Alfred Bloody hell! (*He pays grudgingly*)

Grandma and Elsie enter from the kitchen arch. Grandma is wearing large sun-glasses, an enormous floppy hat and a floral beach-robe. She carries an airbed, not yet inflated. Elsie is dressed in a jazzy summer-weight trouser suit and carries a beach-bag, goggles, snorkel and fishing-net

Alfred chokes over his beer at the sight

Juanito Madre mia!
Alfred You're not going out like that!
Grandma Why not? What's wrong with Norman Hartnell? Come on, Elsie, let's go.

Elsie fumbles in the beach-bag

What are you fiddling about at?
Elsie I just want to be sure I've got everything.
Fritz Don't worry, Fräulein—you have!
Elsie What? (*Suddenly realizing what he means*) Oh! Herr Grotz! Really!
Grandma Now, Herr Grotz! Cut out the flattery. We don't want her head turning.
Fritz But it is true. You are going swimming?
Grandma Not me.
Elsie I'm going diving for shells.
Fritz Shells?

Act I, Scene 2   29

Elsie I'm committed to at least a conch or a scallop for the fifth-form botany class. That's why I've got my snorkel with me.
Fritz I too have a snorkel. Perhaps we can snorkel together—ja?
Mildred You shouldn't go in the sea again, Herr Grotz.
Fritz Vy not?.
Mildred You've only just come out.
Fritz The vater is varm.
Mildred But you haven't finished your drink.
Fritz (*quickly emptying his glass*) I haff now.
Mildred But there are so many English words I want to teach you.
Fritz The time for words is past. Now is the time for action. (*To Elsie*) Fräulein, I am at your service. (*He bows*)
Elsie (*simpering*) It's very kind of you, Herr Grotz.
Fritz It is a pleasure. Ve vill dive together—for a conch—ja?
Elsie Or a scallop . . .
Fritz Or a scallop. Come. (*He leads her to the balcony*) I vill show you the best place. (*He points*) Go to those rocks over there and get ready. I vill join you in a moment—vith my equipment.
Elsie (*giggling*) Oh, I can't wait to tell the fifth-form botany class.

Elsie exits down the steps

Grandma Now just you look here, Herr Grotz . . .
Fritz Please. There is no time. I must get my equipment.
Grandma Elsie's not a strong swimmer.
Fritz Do not vorry. I perform vell on ze vater.
Mildred (*sarcastically*) I'm sure!
Fritz And underneath—I am perfect!

Fritz exits through the kitchen arch

Grandma (*turning to Alfred*) Well?
Alfred Well what?
Grandma What are you sitting there for?
Alfred (*taking a drink from his glass of beer*) I'm having me breakfast.
Grandma Then drink it up and get after her.
Alfred What for?
Grandma To bring her back.
Alfred Aw, come off it, Gran. She's a grown woman. You can't treat her like that.
Grandma I'm not going to stand by while she goes cavorting . . .
Alfred While she goes what?
Grandma Cavorting on the sea bed with that German.
Alfred Don't be stupid. She's only after a few shells.
Grandma She may be. But he isn't.
Alfred For heaven's sake, she's old enough to look after herself.
Grandma That's just what she isn't. I don't know how you can stand by and watch your sister-in-law being seduced . . .

Alfred I'd be hard put to do that without a submarine!
Grandma That settles it! Get me one of them drinks!
Alfred What drinks?
Grandma One of them I had yesterday.
Juanito A Pension Maria Special, señora?
Grandma That's it!
Juanito Pronto, señora. (*He mixes the drinks*)
Grandma (*handing the airbed to Alfred*) And while I'm drinking it you can blow this up for me.
Alfred Me?
Grandma With all that hot air in you it shouldn't be difficult.
Alfred What's the idea?
Grandma Never mind. Get blowing. (*To Mildred*) And as for you, Mildred Armitage, I expect you'll be dying to get back to Jubilee Street.
Mildred Me? What for?
Grandma To tell them all about Elsie's downfall.
Mildred I'm not one to gossip, Mrs Hardcastle. And in any case I quite agree with everything you've just said.
Grandma You do?
Mildred Every word. I wouldn't trust Herr Grotz either.
Grandma It's written all over him, isn't it?
Mildred In big letters. If I was in your shoes I'd do everything to stop him from making a fool of my daughter.
Grandma I'm glad to hear it. Because that's just what I'm going to do.
Alfred You're what? (*He starts to blow*)
Juanito (*serving the drink*) Your Special.
Grandma Thanks.
Mildred Please have it on me.
Grandma That's very kind of you.
Mildred Not at all. (*She pays*)
Grandma Cheers!
Mildred Cheers!

Grandma swallows the drink in one gulp

Grandma (*to Alfred*) Now then? Have you got that thing blown up yet?
Alfred Have a heart. I've only just started.
Grandma Well hurry up. There's no time to waste. You can finish it off on the beach.
Alfred I don't know what's got into you.
Grandma Never mind what's got into me. Stop talking and keep blowing.
Alfred What do you want this thing for anyway?
Grandma To float out on.
Alfred To what?
Grandma To float out on so I can keep them under observation.
Alfred You can't do that.
Grandma Oh yes I can. And you're going to help.
Alfred Me? How?
Grandma By launching me off on it.

Act I, Scene 2   31

Alfred Launching you?
Grandma Well I can't shove off on my own!
Alfred You're mad. You'll drown.
Grandma Not with these I won't. (*She produces a pair of water-wings already inflated from under her beach-robe*) Come on or we'll be too late. (*She shepherds him off*)

Grandma and Alfred exit down the steps

Mildred (*crossing to the bar*) I think this calls for a bottle of champagne, Juanito.
Juanito Champagne, señora?
Mildred In England no launching ceremony is complete without it.
Juanita Then try this, señora. (*He produces a bottle*) Perelada . . . fifty pesetas.
Mildred Fine. (*She pays*)

Fritz enters from the kitchen arch. He is wearing flippers, goggles and a snorkel, one end of which is in his mouth

Juanito pours out a glass of champagne as Fritz moves to the centre of the patio

   (*Picking up the bottle*) Herr Grotz!
Fritz (*turning and speaking in a muffled voice through the snorkel*) Ja?
Mildred (*crossing to him with the bottle of champagne*) For you.
Fritz (*still in a muffled voice*) Was is das?
Mildred (*pouring champagne down his snorkel*) Champers. And I hope it chokes you!

It does. Spluttering, Fritz pulls off his goggles and snorkel

Fritz (*expostulating*) Frau Armitage dat vas—(*he suddenly recognizes the taste of champagne and his tone quickly changes*)—dat vas champagne!
Mildred That's right. Have another. (*She hands him a glass*)
Fritz No, please, I haff to go—I . . . (*The proferred glass is too tempting for him. He takes it*) Danke.
Mildred A pleasure, I'm sure. I always think champagne goes with—er—romance. Don't you?
Fritz Ja. (*Referring to the champagne*) It is good.
Mildred Romance?
Fritz Ja. Dat is good too.
Mildred Especially on holiday. When one is so much more relaxed as you might say.
Fritz Ja.
Mildred Do sit down and have another.

Fritz sits. Mildred turns away from him and starts to refill his glass at the bar. Juanito moves up the bar out of earshot. Fritz crosses his legs, and the tip of his flipper touches Mildred's bottom. She freezes but does not turn round

(*With assumed coyness*) Herr Grotz!
Fritz (*unaware of what he has done*) Ja?
Mildred Not here!

Fritz uncrosses his legs and touches her again. She turns

I said not here!
Fritz (*still not understanding*) Vot is not here?
Mildred Not in front of Juanito!
Fritz Vot must I not do?
Mildred Oh, don't look so innocent!
Fritz But vot haff I done?
Mildred You nipped me!
Fritz I nipped you?
Mildred Yes.
Fritz Where?
Mildred Really, Herr Grotz! Juanito's listening.
Fritz But I do not understand. Vere did I nip you?
Mildred Well maybe it wasn't exactly a nip . . .
Fritz Then vot vas it?
Mildred (*hopefully*) More of a —tickle, perhaps?
Fritz (*sternly*) You say I am tickling you?
Mildred Oh come off it. Don't act so innocent!
Fritz (*coldly*) I do not nip or tickle in public!
Mildred Oh yes you do!
Fritz Oh no I do not!
Mildred You jolly well did!
Fritz I jolly vell did not!
Mildred You touched my bottom!
Fritz I did not!
Mildred Oh yes you did!
Fritz (*on his dignity*) The only thing I haff touched of yours is your champagne. And that—like your bottom—is flat!
Mildred Really!
Fritz Good day!

Fritz stalks off down the steps

Mildred Blast!
Juanito It was his flipper, señora.
Mildred His what?
Juanito His flipper. When he crossed his legs.
Mildred Oh no! (*She runs to the top of the steps*) Herr Grotz!

Mildred follows Fritz off down the steps

Juanito shrugs, comes from behind the bar; and starts to clear up

Gloria enters from the kitchen arch and sits at the bar

Act I, Scene 2

Juanito Buenas dias, señorita.
Gloria It's not "buenas" as far as I'm concerned.
Juanito The sun is shining.
Gloria I don't care.
Juanito You must not be unhappy in Pension Maria, señorita. I will give you something to cheer you up. (*He goes behind the bar and starts to pour out a stiff brandy*)
Gloria Nothing'll cheer me up. Not after what I've gone through.
Juanito (*putting the glass in front of her*) Drink this. With my compliments. It will make you feel better. ·
Gloria (*drinking it in one gulp*) It didn't.

He pours a second drink. She lifts the glass. He restrains her

Juanito Not so quick this time.

She takes a sip

Gloria Are you married?
Juanito I will be next year, señorita.·
Gloria Then you're engaged to someone?
Juanito Yes.
Gloria Tell me—what would you do if you caught her messing about with someone else?
Juanito I would kill him.
Gloria You would?
Juanito Naturally.
Gloria (*finishing off the second brandy and beginning to feel it*) I don't think I could do that.
Juanito Of course not. You are a woman.
Gloria I might scratch her eyes out.
Juanito You have someone who has done this to you?
Gloria Right here.
Juanito Here?
Gloria In this bar?
Juanito When?
Gloria This morning.
Juanito Who is this woman?
Gloria Your barmaid.
Juanito My what?
Gloria Rosita.
Juanito Madre mia!
Gloria What's the matter?
Juanito Tell me, who is your man?
Gloria Ron.

Juanito picks up the knife he uses for cutting lemons and savagely cuts a lemon in half

You'd better put that down or you'll do yourself an injury. (*With sudden realization*) Hey, wait a minute, Rosita isn't your ...?

Juanito I will kill him.
Gloria Now hold on a bit...
Juanito If you are telling me the truth...
Gloria Of course I'm telling you the truth. But you mustn't kill him.
Juanito Why not?
Gloria Well not immediately.
Juanito The quicker the better.
Gloria Not until he's been taught a lesson.
Juanito There is only one lesson I will teach him.
Gloria Hang on a tick. I've got an idea...
Juanito I torture him first?
Gloria No—I mean yes.
Juanito How?
Gloria Well, supposing that when he comes in here—you and me were—er...
Juanito Were what?
Gloria Well, you know, kissing and...
Juanito And what?
Gloria That's up to you isn't it?
Juanito He might kill me.
Gloria He wouldn't do that. We don't do those sort of things in England.
Juanito (*suddenly interested*) No? Then that is good. (*He drinks a brandy quickly*)
Gloria Then it's OK by you...?

Juanito emerges quickly from behind the bar and embraces her

Hey! What's the idea?
Juanito There is someone coming. It is probably him. (*He starts to kiss her passionately*)

Rosita enters from the kitchen arch. She carries a tray of bottles and glasses

Assessing the situation, Rosita puts the tray down on a table, picks up one of the bottles and is about to hit Juanito over the head with it

Ron enters up the parapet steps

Ron Rosita! What on earth...?

Rosita lowers the bottle, replaces it, and goes to Ron. Gloria and Juanito, in a deep embrace, are unaware of what is going on

And to think she had the flipping nerve to accuse me...

He is unable to finish what he is saying as Rosita embraces him and starts to kiss him passionately. He is too surprised to react with enthusiasm to begin with, but after a few seconds his attitude changes. They break. He is now a little breathless

Act I, Scene 2   35

   Madre mia!

Ron now grabs Rosita with enthusiasm and they again kiss passionately. Gloria and Juanito break, and for the first time they see Rosita and Ron

Juanito You are quite right, señorita! I will kill him! (*He dives back behind the bar and picks up the knife. He attempts to cross to Ron and Rosita*)
Gloria (*restraining him*) No!
Juanito I will kill them both!
Gloria Wait!

   Mildred enters up the steps

Mildred Well!
Gloria Well what?
Mildred He's at it again!

Rosita and Ron break. Juanito tries to get to Rosita but Gloria restrains him

Juanito Mujer perfida! Matare os ambos!
Rosita Me? Perfida? Es usted qui es perfido! Deme ese cuchillo!
Juanito (*flourishing the knife*) No!
Rosita (*avoiding Ron's attempt to restrain her and picking up the bottle*) En tal caso te golpare con esta botella!

Juanito pushes past Gloria and advances on Rosita with the knife. Rosita raises the bottle threateningly

Gloria Stop them! For heaven's sake stop them!
Mildred (*in an authoritative voice*) Juanito!
Juanito (*reacting automatically and taking a few steps towards her*) Señora?

Rosita seizes her opportunity while Juanito's attention is momentarily distracted and brings the bottle down smartly on his head. He collapses in a sitting position on a chair. Becoming suddenly repentant, Rosita runs forward, supports him and attempts to revive him

Rosita Amanti mi!

   Fritz enters up the steps carrying an unconscious Elsie. A net bag full of shells and sea urchins hangs from his arm

Mildred Oh my Gawd! What's happened to her?
Fritz She has fainted.
Mildred What did you do to her?
Fritz I saved her!
Mildred From what?
Fritz An octopus!
Mildred Put her down! Over there!

Fritz dumps Elsie in a sitting position in a chair at the same table as Juanito

   And get her a brandy.

Rosita Si, señora. (*She runs to the bar*)

Fritz props Elsie back to back with the unconscious Juanito so that they support each other

Fritz (*crossing to Mildred*) It had the biggest tentacles I haff ever seen.
Mildred Never mind about it's tentacles!
Fritz But they were that big! (*He opens his arms wide. The net swings out and narrowly misses Mildred*)
Mildred Hey, watch it! You nearly hit me with that thing!
Fritz I am sorry.
Mildred What is it?
Fritz Her collection of shells and ur-chins! Sea ur-chins!
Mildred Never mind the English lesson. Get rid of it. (*Fritz tosses the net bag of shells and sea urchins on to a chair*) Hurry up with that brandy. And make it two while you're at it.
Rosita Si, señora.

Alfred and Nora enter up the steps carrying Grandma

Mildred Oh my Gawd!
Alfred Well, give us a hand, someone.

Ron and Fritz rush forward to assist

Mildred Make it three brandies, Rosita.
Rosita Si, señora.

Ron and Fritz lay Grandma on the bench. Nora sits on the end of the bench supporting her head

Mildred What happened to her?
Alfred She slipped.
Nora Off her lilo.
Alfred Went down like a stone.
Nora And nearly drowned.
Alfred She'd be a gonner by now if I hadn't rescued her.
Mildred From the look of her I'm not sure she isn't.
Nora (*suddenly anxious*) Oh no!
Mildred I don't want to worry you but it costs a packet getting a dear departed back to U.K.
Nora Alfred. Do something!
Alfred What?
Nora Revive her! Give her the kiss of life!
Alfred You must be joking!
Nora I mean it! Go on, kiss her!
Alfred I'm not playing postman's knock with your blooming mother!

Grandma groans

Nora She's coming to!
Alfred Thank God for that!

Act I, Scene 2

Grandma groans again

Nora She's trying to say something. (*Bending over Grandma*) Speak to me, Mother! Say something! She can't hear me!
Alfred Come here, let me try! (*He kneels down at the other side of Grandma and pats her hand*) Come on, Gran, love. Whatever it is, let's have it!

Grandma ejects a jet of water all over Alfred

Bloody hell!
Nora Shut up! We can't hear what she's trying to tell us. What is it, Mum?

Grandma gives a gurgle and tries to speak

She's lost her voice.
Grandma It isn't me voice I've lost, it's me teeth!
Alfred Oh my Gawd!

Alfred starts to laugh, and sits in the chair on top of the shells and sea urchins. His laughter changes to a look of agony, as—

the CURTAIN *falls*

ACT II
Scene 1

The same. The following lunch-time

When the Curtain rises, Juanito is behind the bar drying glasses. Alfred is standing at the bar eating the first course of his lunch. Rosita enters from the dining-room carrying Alfred's second course. She gives Juanito a haughty look. There is obviously still tension between them

Rosita Are you ready for the next course, señor?
Alfred No.
Rosita I will come back. (*She turns to go*)
Alfred Don't go. I've had enough of this rabbit food. (*He pushes his plate away*) What's this, then? Oh, not bloody fish again!
Rosita You do not like fish, señor?
Alfred If it's done in batter with a few chips round it.
Rosita It is very fresh, señor...
Alfred Looks dead drunk to me with them glazed eyes. Take it away. I can't bear to look at it.
Rosita I will bring you your sweet. (*She picks up the dish*) You like melon?

Nora enters from the dining-room holding her napkin. She is in the middle of her lunch

Alfred Not if it's that red stuff with black beetles in it.
Rosita Crême caramel then, señor.
Alfred All right. I'll try it.

Rosita exits to the dining-room

Nora And I hope you'll change your mind and have it in the dining-room in a civilized fashion.
Alfred You know very well I can't.
Nora If you can eat in here you can eat in there.
Alfred But I can't sit down, can I?
Nora I don't see why not.
Alfred You would if you had a backside full of prickles.
Nora They'd give you a cushion if you asked for it.
Alfred It's no good. I've tried it. I'd have to stand in there just like I'm standing here.
Nora Well, at least you'd be sociable.
Alfred Have some sense. I'd feel a proper Charlie with all that lot staring at me.

Act II, Scene 1 39

Nora And how do you think I feel? You eating in here and me eating out there. Goodness knows what people are thinking.
Alfred Then put them out of their misery and tell them.
Nora Don't be ridiculous.
Alfred Why not? All you've got to do is stand up and shout "Please excuse my husband. He can't come in and sit down because he's got a bum full of prickles."
Nora For heaven's sake keep your voice down. They'll hear you.
Alfred It'll save you having to tell them then, won't it?
Nora You don't know what it's like in there sitting on your own. Putting up with their funny glances.
Alfred You're not sitting on your own. You've got the rest of the family with you.
Nora No, I haven't. Ron didn't come down to lunch and Elsie's spent the whole time giggling and making eyes at that German.
Alfred What about Grandma?
Nora She's sitting there trying to chew with her teeth out.
Alfred Hard luck.
Nora Well, are you coming back in or aren't you?
Alfred No. Until I can sit in comfort I'm having all my meals out here at the bar.
Nora I don't know why you're making such a fuss. You've had boils there before.
Alfred Boils aren't prickles!
Nora Then I think you'd better see a doctor.
Alfred What could he do?
Nora Pull them out. Or maybe it's a job for a dentist.
Alfred Doctors? Dentists? We're not on the National Health here, you know.
Nora That doesn't matter. We're insured against accident, sickness and death.
Alfred Oh, are we?
Nora What do you mean, "Oh, are we?" You ought to know. You paid the travel agent's account.
Alfred So I did.
Nora You didn't forget to pay the insurance, did you? (*Pause*) Well, did you?
Alfred It were an optional extra.
Nora Trust you!
Alfred Well, ten pounds is a lot of money.
Nora I'd pay more than that to sit down in comfort.
Alfred Of course you would. You don't have to earn it. All you do is spend it.

Rosita enters from the dining-room with a plate

Rosita (*placing Alfred's sweet in front of him*) Your crême caramel, señor.
Alfred Oh, thank you.

Rosita (*to Nora*) Your sweet is on the table, señora.
Nora Thanks.

Rosita exits to the dining-room

Well, if you're not coming, I'm going back. (*She stands waiting for him to change his mind*)
Alfred Well, go on, then.
Nora All right, I will.

Fritz enters from the dining-room and pauses just behind Nora

(*Not noticing Fritz*) But for heaven's sake have a bit of sense. Get someone to look at that bottom of yours. (*She turns to go and almost collides with Fritz*) Oh, Herr Grotz, I'm sorry. I didn't see you. I was just telling . . . Excuse me.

Nora exits to the dining-room

Fritz Good afternoon, Herr Tinsley.
Alfred Afternoon.
Fritz You haff finished your lunch?
Alfred No.
Fritz I was just going to ask you to join me in a glass of cognac.
Alfred (*pushing his plate away*) I've finished.
Fritz That is good. Two cognacs, Juanito.
Juanito Ja, mein Herr.
Fritz Cognac is good for the digestion, ja?
Alfred It's good for anything.
Juanito Two cognacs, mein Herr.
Fritz Danke.
Alfred (*picking up his brandy*) Cheers!
Fritz (*lifting his glass*) Up with the bottom!
Alfred I beg your pardon?
Fritz Is that not vot you say in England ven you drink?
Alfred No, it isn't. We say "bottoms up".
Fritz Ah, I am sorry. I haff got the bottom wrong.
Alfred You're not the only one. I can't even sit on mine.
Fritz Ah! Of course! Now I understand. The sea-urchins?
Alfred Right.
Fritz The prickles are still vith you?
Alfred They're not only with me, they're in me.
Fritz But you must remove them at once.
Alfred I haven't got eyes in the back of me head.
Fritz But sometimes they are poisonous. They must come out.
Alfred Poisonous? Oh, my God! Juanito, give me a double brandy and then get me a doctor.
Juanito Very good, señor.

Act II, Scene 1   41

Fritz Do not be hasty, Herr Tinsley. A doctor is not necessary. If you vill allow me . . .
Alfred Allow you . . . ?
Fritz I am a medical man.
Alfred A doctor?
Fritz I have studied medicine.
Alfred Oh, well, then. (*To Juanito*) Give a double brandy to Doctor Grotz, Juanito.
Juanito A moment, please, señor. I get another bottle.

Juanito exits to the dining-room

Alfred Now then . . .
Fritz You are lucky. I haff my tweezers with me. (*He takes a pair of tweezers out of his pocket*) Now, where is the trouble?
Alfred Trouble? Well, it's on me . . . (*He whispers the rest*)
Fritz Where?
Alfred On my . . . (*He whispers*)
Fritz Speak up, please.
Alfred On me right cheek.
Fritz Oh.
Alfred (*softly*) Just under the—er . . . (*He traces a curve in the air with his hand*)
Fritz That is good.
Alfred Good?
Fritz Plenty of flesh for the prickles to bed into. Take down your trousers.
Alfred What?
Fritz Undo your pants.
Alfred Here?
Fritz It will only take a minute.
Alfred I can't take them off in here.
Fritz Do you want to be poisoned?
Alfred But someone might come in.
Fritz Then go behind the bar.
Alfred (*doing as instructed*) I don't like this a bit.
Fritz Hurry up! Juanito will be back. (*He sits on the bar*)
Alfred Well, I've got 'em off. What now? (*He drapes his trousers over the bar*)
Fritz (*leaning over the bar*) Bend down.
Alfred I suppose you *are* a medical man. (*He bends down out of sight*)

Mildred enters from the dining-room

Mildred Ah! Herr Grotz!

Fritz nearly falls off the bar. Mildred rushes forward and helps to pull him back

Whatever are you doing?

Fritz I was getting my glass. It fell off the bar.
Mildred I was looking for you.
Fritz You vos?
Mildred Yes. I want to apologize.
Fritz To me?
Mildred Yes. I know now that you didn't.
Fritz Didn't vot?
Mildred Do what I thought you did.
Fritz Vot did I thought you did?
Mildred Not you, me. I thought it was you, but it wasn't.
Fritz Who vos it, then?
Mildred It was your flipper.
Fritz Oh.
Mildred Juanito told me.
Fritz He did?
Mildred Yes. And just between you and me I wouldn't have said anything at all if we'd been alone.
Fritz You wouldn't?
Mildred No. But one has to keep up appearances. Especially in front of foreigners.
Fritz Foreigners?
Mildred (*hastily*) I mean—Spaniards.
Fritz Ah!
Mildred (*looking around*) But now that there's no-one else about. Just you and me alone. (*Sidling up to him in a seductive fashion*) You won't find me—unresponsive. (*She stands provocatively close to him*) Well? Don't just stand there staring. What's the matter with you?
Fritz I have a problem.
Mildred A problem?
Fritz Ja. One I must get to the bottom of.
Mildred (*suspiciously*) Really?
Fritz The fact is I am busy at the moment. You understand?
Mildred I'm not sure that I do. (*She sees Alfred's trousers draped over the counter*) Are these your trousers?
Fritz No—I mean, ja.
Mildred What are they doing on the bar?
Fritz I put them there.
Mildred It's a funny place to put a pair of trousers.
Fritz Ja, I know, but you see . . . (*He falters*)
Mildred I don't.
Fritz Well, I brought them with me to—er—to give to someone . . .
Mildred Yes?
Fritz To give to someone willing to sew a button on them for me.
Mildred Oh, well, if that's your problem it's easily solved. Allow me. (*She picks up the trousers*) I'll just pop them along to my room. (*She turns to go*)
Fritz No!
Mildred (*turning*) Don't you want me to solve your problem for you?

Act II, Scene 1   43

Fritz Well, yes, but . . .
Mildred That's all right, then. I won't be long. And maybe when I come back we can go for a little walk round the bay together.

Mildred exits through the kitchen arch

Alfred reappears and comes from behind the bar wearing long underpants

Alfred Of all the stupid things to do! Letting that woman run off with my pants.
Fritz I am sorry.
Alfred I should blooming well think so. I can't leave this place now. I'm a prisoner!
Fritz A prisoner at the bar, ja?
Alfred Don't try and be funny. Get those damn prickles out quick!
Fritz I can't while you're wearing those things.
Alfred Now wait a minute—there are limits.
Fritz Do you wish to die of poison?
Alfred No.
Fritz Then get back behind the bar quick and take off your ballet trousers before someone comes.

Fritz bustles Alfred back behind the bar protesting. The pants come off and are put in a bundle on the bar

Alfred I feel a right Charlie.
Fritz Bend over that stool.

Alfred bends over

   Now grind your teeth.
Alfred You mean grit 'em.

Fritz starts to take out the first prickle

   Ouch!

Ron enters through the kitchen arch. He approaches the bar curiously

Ron My God, what's that?
Alfred (*reacting*) Who the devil . . . ? (*Another prickle comes out*) Ouch!
Ron Oh, it's you, Dad.
Alfred Of course it's me.
Ron I thought for one moment you were a hedgehog.
Alfred Very funny! Ouch!
Fritz That vos a big one.
Ron Have you seen Gloria?
Alfred No, I haven't. (*To Fritz*) Have you finished?
Fritz Four more to go.
Alfred Ouch!
Fritz Three.

Alfred (*to Ron*) If you want to make yourself useful go and get my trousers back from that woman.
Ron What woman?
Alfred Your future mother-in-law.
Ron I'll not do that.
Alfred Why?
Ron We're not on speaking terms.
Alfred Ouch! That hurt!
Fritz Only one more.

Ron moves towards the dining-room

Alfred (*to Ron*) Where are you going?
Ron To find Gloria. To have it out with her.
Alfred That can wait. There's a job for you here.
Ron What sort of a job?
Alfred Smuggling me out of this place without pants. Ouch!
Fritz And that's the last one.
Alfred Thank God for that. Now, when I've got me underpants on you two stand by me. One in front and one behind...

Voices are heard from the dining-room

Ron You'll never do it. There's someone coming.
Alfred Damn and blast. Take cover.

Ron joins Fritz behind the bar and they pull Alfred down out of sight

Gloria enters from the dining-room followed by Juanito who is carrying a bottle of brandy which he puts on the bar. Gloria sits at one of the tables

Juanito But no-one will know. Tonight when I am off duty you will come to my room—yes?
Gloria I will come to your room—no!
Juanito But, señorita, I wish to show you the big passion I have for you.
Gloria You can keep that to yourself.

Ron's head appears above the bar

Juanito But my heart—it is full of love!

Ron is about to speak. Alfred and Fritz appear on either side of him and pull him down out of sight

Gloria That is what all you hot-blooded Latins say.
Juanito It is true.
Gloria And if I believed you I'd finish up like Maisie Arkwright.
Juanito Who is Maisie Arkwright?
Gloria Friend of mine. Spent last summer in San Antonio. And look what happened...
Juanito What did happen?
Gloria There was this Spanish waiter who kept making sheep's eyes at her.
Juanito So?

Act II, Scene 1   45

Gloria She came back with one in the oven.
Juanito A sheep's eye?
Gloria No. She was in the club.
Juanito Golf?
Gloria No. Pudding.
Juanito Pudding club?
Gloria Look, let's start again. She was preggers.
Juanito (*blankly*) Oh.
Gloria Bambino—chicito—savvy?
Juanito (*understanding at last*) Ah! Si, si! (*A slight pause*) You wish for one, too?
Gloria Me? Of all the cheek!
Juanito Later, perhaps.
Gloria Not even later—Don Juanito!
Juanito But when we are married—yes?
Gloria When we are *what*?
Juanito Permit me to speak, señorita. I have made a big decision.
Gloria Really? And what's that?
Juanito I will not kill him.
Gloria Who?
Juanito Your Ron. If he wants Rosita he can have her. And I will have you.
Gloria Like hell you will.
Juanito (*falling on his knees beside her*) Señorita—please—I love you—I will do anything for you.
Gloria Then get off your knees for a start.
Juanito Pronto, señorita.
Gloria And pour me a drink.
Juanito What do you wish? (*He half turns towards the bar*)
Gloria I think I'll have a beer.

Quick as a flash the bottle of brandy is whisked away and replaced by a bottle of beer

No, wait, make it a citron.

A bottle of lemonade is substituted for the beer. Juanito goes to the bar. He turns back to Gloria as she speaks

On second thoughts I'll have a beer after all.

A bottle of beer is substituted for the lemonade. Juanito is about to go behind the bar when he notices the beer. He picks it up and looks at it in a puzzled fashion. Satisfied that it is beer, he goes back to Gloria with it

Juanito One beer, señorita. (*He takes an opener from his jacket and removes the beer-cap. Gazing at her intently, he places the beer before her on the table*)

Gloria looks at Juanito, then at the beer, with a quizzical expression

So sorry, señorita. A glass, of course.

A glass immediately appears on the bar. Juanito turns towards the bar and is surprised at the sight of it. He pauses for a moment, then shrugs and picks it up. He returns to Gloria and starts to pour out the beer, gazing fondly at her as he does so

Gloria I wish you'd stop looking at me like that.
Juanito I cannot help it. You are so beautiful. I hope you do not resent the urge I have to put my eyes upon you.
Gloria Just as long as it doesn't spread to your hands.
Juanito My hands are trembling with your nearness.
Gloria Then keep the damn things steady. You're spilling the beer.
Juanito Señorita! I am so sorry! (*He crosses to the bar and picks up Alfred's underpants*)
Gloria (*jumping up*) Of all the clumsy idiots. I'm soaked!
Juanito Please allow me to rub you. (*Using the underpants he starts to mop her skirt*)
Gloria Oh, give that to me. (*She snatches the pants from Juanito*)

Rosita enters from the kitchen arch

The legs of the pants unroll

Oh!
Rosita So!
Juanito They are not mine.
Gloria Oh! (*She throws the pants angrily at Juanito, who catches them*)

Gloria storms off down the steps

Juanito Eres muy estupida!
Rosita No soy. Eres muy estupido y muy perfido!
Juanito No soy perfido. No amo la muchacha inglesa. Te amo!
Rosita No me amas! No amas la muchacha inglesa cualquira! Te amas! Te! Te!
Juanito (*attempting to embrace her*) Te monstrare que te amo.
Rosita (*pushing him away*) Te paras! No me tocas!
Juanito Por que?
Rosita Por que no te amo.
Juanito Rosita, con permiso de te——
Rosita No! Nunca mas!

Elsie enters from the dining-room, followed by Nora

Nora Elsie! Come back!
Elsie I won't!
Nora But we can't leave Grandma on her own in the dining-room.
Elsie I can. I've had enough of watching her eat without teeth...
Nora Have a heart. Her spare set hurts.
Elsie Then why can't she leave them out all the time? Instead of putting them in between courses.

Act II, Scene 1

Grandma enters from the dining-room

Grandma What's the idea of leaving me on my own?
Nora Well, we'd finished and Elsie wanted a breath of air and——
Elsie I didn't. I wanted to get out before you put your teeth back in in front of everybody.
Grandma And what's wrong with that?
Elsie It's not polite. You could at least put 'em in behind your hanky.
Grandma Teeth is teeth. Either you've got 'em or you haven't. And I haven't. Not me proper ones, anyway.
Nora Don't keep on about your teeth, Mother.
Grandma I can't help it. With all this strange food and nothing to chew it with, I'll have stomach trouble for the rest of me life.
Nora I've brought your Rennies.
Grandma They're no good if you haven't masticated your food properly.

Juanito pulls out a chair for her to sit on

Thank you, young man. I'll have two coffees, please.
Nora But there's three of us.
Grandma Then order your own. I need two if I can't get solid nourishment.
Nora (*sitting on the bench*) Four coffees, please, Juanito.
Juanito Certainly, señorita. Rosita!

Rosita glares at him, tosses her head, and exits through the kitchen arch

Please excuse me. (*He starts to wipe the table with the underpants*)

Alfred's head appears above the bar and watches the ensuing scene anxiously. One of the legs of the pants unrolls

Elsie What's that you're wiping the table with?
Juanito What? Oh, excuse me. (*He tucks the leg up quickly*) I . . .
Elsie It's a pair of underpants.
Juanito I am sorry. I make a mistake.
Nora I should think so too.
Grandma Fancy using your pants to wipe the table . . .
Juanito They are not mine.
Grandma I don't fancy my coffee off that table now.
Juanito But they are quite clean.
Grandma How do you know, if they are not yours?
Juanito Well, you see—I—er—found them.
Nora Found them?
Juanito On the terrace—this morning.
Grandma Did you find a pair of drawers, 'n all?
Nora Mother, please!
Juanito No, you do not understand. They have been dropped.
Grandma You don't say?
Juanito From the balcony of the bedroom over the dining-room.

Grandma Thrown off?
Juanito No. Blown off. They had been hung to dry. That is why they must be clean.
Grandma And that's why I know they aren't Alfred's.
Nora And just what do you mean by that?
Grandma Well, they can't be his, can they? Your bedroom isn't over the dining-room.
Nora No. Although it had crossed my mind...
Grandma Mine, too. There aren't many folk who'd wear daft things like that in a climate like this.
Juanito Excuse me, I will get another cloth.

Alfred's head disappears as Juanito turns

Juanito exits through the kitchen arch, carrying the pants
Elsie sits on the bench and starts to giggle

Nora What's the matter with you?
Elsie I'm just trying to imagine Mildred Armitage in those underpants.
Nora Why bother to do that?
Elsie Well, they must be hers.
Nora Hers?
Elsie They blew off her balcony. She has the bedroom over the dining-room.
Nora (*as a sobering thought strikes her*) Oh, good Lord! I've just had a horrible thought. I think I'll have a closer look at them pants. What's he done with them?
Elsie He's taken them with him.
Grandma I don't know why you're bothering about a pair of underpants. It's my teeth you should be worrying about.
Nora Oh, for heaven's sake, Mother, stop moaning about your teeth. If you'd kept your mouth shut in the first place you wouldn't have lost them.
Grandma I wouldn't have lost them if I'd gone to Blackpool...
Nora Here we go again. Don't you think we've had enough?
Grandma I've had enough—of these spares. They're giving me gumboils.
Nora Then leave them out.
Grandma And a fine sight I'd look gumming me way through me meals for the rest of me holiday.
Elsie You can always stick to the soup.
Grandma Or go home. (*She gets up*)
Nora Don't be silly, Mother, you'd never get on a plane by yourself.
Grandma Then there's only one alternative. I've got to find me old set.
Nora Impossible.
Grandma No, it isn't. I know roughly where they are. Near the rocks where Elsie picked up her sea urchins.
Nora You'll never find them.
Grandma I'll get Fritz to dive for me.
Nora You can't ask him to do that.

Act II, Scene 1

Grandma Why not?
Nora Well, just look at the weather. There's a storm blowing up.

Alfred, holding a bar tray in front of him, edges out from behind the bar. Fritz and Ron follow him out and, standing side by side, they hide the three women's view of him. Very slowly they all three start to move to the exit to the dining-room

Grandma Storms don't worry me.
Nora They do when there's thunder.
Grandma Don't talk rubbish. Thunder doesn't frighten me.

Alfred drops the tray, which falls with a crash

(*Reacting in terror*) My Gawd! What's that?

Alfred dashes back behind the bar. Ron picks up the tray as Grandma turns and sees him and Fritz

That's a daft trick to play on anyone, Ronald Tinsley! Consider yourself lucky I didn't drop down dead with a corona trombonist.
Ron I'm sorry, Grandma. It was an accident.

Juanito enters with a clean teacloth

Grandma Then put that tray down before you have another.

Ron hands the tray to Juanito, who puts it on the bar and places the teacloth beside it. Fritz turns to go

Oh, Mr Grotz! Fritz! Don't go! I've something I want to have a word with you about. And you, Juanito.
Juanito Me, señora?
Grandma Yes, both of you.
Fritz (*clicking his heels*) I am at your service, Fräu Hardcastle.
Grandma Well—er—you probably both know that when I fell in the water yesterday I—er—lost part of myself.
Juanito Ah! Your—er—top, I suppose?
Grandma And me bottom.
Juanito So you are wanting another—er—swimming costume?
Grandma I'm talking about me top and bottom set.
Juanito What is your set?
Grandma Me teeth!
Juanito (*understanding*) Ah!
Nora Out there—on the reef.
Fritz But, mein frau, your mouth is full of them.
Grandma Them's me spares. And they hurt. Me comfy ones are somewhere out there. And I want them back.
Juanito But, señora, it is not easy to find such things ...
Grandma I know where they are. All I need is a boat, someone to row, and someone to dive.
Fritz (*patting himself on the chest*) Frau Hardcastle, you haff your diver!
Grandma That's what I hoped you'd say.

Elsie And I'll go with him.
Grandma You'll do no such thing.
Elsie But with two of us looking we'll find them quicker.
Grandma There was enough hanky-panky going on under the water yesterday. Where's Alfred?
Nora Snoring on his back upstairs, I should imagine.
Grandma Then it'll have to be Ron.
Ron What will?
Grandma The oarsman.
Ron You haven't got a boat yet.
Grandma I will have. Won't I, Juanito?
Juanito Señora?
Grandma What about borrowing your father's boat?
Juanito That is not easy, señora.
Grandma It had better be. Otherwise Sunkissed Tours will get a very unfavourable report about this place.
Juanito But the weather, señora. There is going to be a storm.
Grandma Nothing to the one I'll raise if I don't get that boat.
Juanito I will go and ask my father.

Juanito exits through the kitchen arch

Grandma Right. Now then, if you insist upon coming with us, Elsie, you'd better go and get yourself ready.
Elsie You mean I can go?
Grandma Yes. On second thoughts my teeth are more important than your virtue.
Nora I don't think any of you ought to go. If the storm comes on when you're all out there ...
Grandma We'll be ready for it. (*To Elsie*) Pop in the kitchen on your way, Elsie, and tell Juanito we want to borrow his father's oilskins as well as his boat.
Elsie Right.

Elsie exits through the kitchen arch, passing Rosita who is entering with a tray of coffee

Grandma Ah, the coffee! At last! Put it over here.

Rosita places the tray on the coffee-table in front of Nora and Grandma. Grandma turns to Ron, who is leaning over the bar and making furtive signs to Alfred

Do you want a cup of coffee Ron? I haven't time to drink my second cup.
Ron What? Oh, no. No thanks, Gran.
Grandma Then go and get ready. (*To Fritz*) And if you're going to do some diving you'd better go and get your snitzel. (*She drinks her coffee*)
Fritz At once, Frau Hardcastle.

Fritz clicks his heels and, after giving an anxious glance at the bar, exits through the kitchen arch. Ron follows him off

Act II, Scene 1   51

Grandma (*to Nora*) And you'd better hurry up or the others'll be ready before you.

Rosita exits through the kitchen arch with the tray of coffee cups

Nora I'm not coming with you.
Grandma Yes, you are. I've got a job for you.
Nora Wild horses wouldn't drag me into that boat.
Grandma I don't want you on the boat. I want you on the beach.
Nora On the beach?
Grandma Looking out.
Nora For what?
Grandma Danger.
Nora That's ridiculous.
Grandma No, it isn't. You never know what might be lurking about in these foreign seas. Giant octopussies, Russian submarines . . . anything.

Juanito enters from the kitchen arch carrying oilskins and sou'westers

Well?
Juanito My father is unhappy about the boat. It is only insured for fishing for fish not fishing for teeth.
Grandma And how much does he want to make him happy?
Juanito Five hundred pesetas.
Grandma Done! Add it to Mr Tinsley's bill.

Alfred's head appears above the bar

Juanito He says you must go quickly. Before the storm. The sky is very black.

Alfred's head disappears

Grandma We'll be off in a minute when the others are ready.

Elsie enters from the kitchen arch. She is apparently wearing nothing but a long polo-necked jersey

You're not going to dive in that!
Elsie No, I'll take it off.
Grandma You'll what?
Elsie I've got my bikini on underneath. (*She lifts up the front of her jumper to demonstrate*)

Fritz enters from the dining-room carrying his diving gear. He looks at Elsie's demonstration

Elsie realizes, and quickly pulls the jumper down

Grandma Where's Ron?

Ron enters through the kitchen arch, also dressed in a long woolly

Ron I'm here.
Grandma Right, then let's go.
Juanito I will take you to the boat.

Juanito exits down the steps, followed by Grandma, Nora, Ron and Elsie

Fritz is about to follow

Mildred enters through the kitchen arch, carrying the trousers

Mildred Oh—Fritz!
Fritz (*turning*) Frau Armitage?
Mildred About your flies.
Fritz I am not going fishing.
Mildred No, I mean these. (*She holds up the trousers*) There's no button missing.

Alfred's head appears above the bar

Fritz No?

Elsie reappears on the steps

Elsie Come on, Fritz. Hurry.
Fritz Ja. Please excuse us. We must get down to it before the storm comes.
Mildred Really! (*Throwing the trousers at him angrily*) Your trousers!
Fritz (*bowing*) Your pardon!

Fritz exits with Elsie down the steps, carrying the diving tackle and the trousers

Mildred turns in anger to the bar, and sees Alfred

Alfred I think you could do with a double brandy.
Mildred You can say that again. (*He pours one out for her*) Of all the two-timing, ungrateful . . .
Alfred There. (*He places the brandy in front of her*) Put that down and you'll feel better.
Mildred (*after drinking it in one gulp*) Do you know what he did?
Alfred No.
Mildred Tried to get me to sew a button on a zip fastener.
Alfred He didn't?
Mildred He did. And do you know why?
Alfred No.
Mildred To get me out of the way. To give him a clear run with that sister-in-law of yours.
Alfred Mm. Have another.
Mildred I shouldn't.
Alfred On me this time. (*He tops up her glass*)

Act II, Scene 1   53

Mildred You know, you're not such a bad sort.
Alfred I know.
Mildred The only thing that's wrong with you is your family.
Alfred They're all right. You've just got to get used to them. Like rheumatism. You don't notice it after you've had it a year or two.
Mildred I'd never get used to your family.
Alfred You might have to if your Gloria and our Ron patch up their quarrel.
Mildred They'll never do that.
Alfred I wouldn't be too sure. Have another drop. (*He tops up her glass*)
Mildred Mr Tinsley! You'll be having me tiddly!
Alfred That's the idea.
Mildred What?
Alfred Would you rather have beer?
Mildred No, I never mix drinks.
Alfred Very sensible.
Mildred (*the alcohol taking effect*) You know, I can feel this. Have a cigarette. (*She brings a packet from her handbag and offers one*)
Alfred No, thanks, I'll stick to my pipe.

Mildred produces a lighter and tries to light her cigarette. The lighter slips out of her fingers and falls behind the bar

Mildred Damn! I've dropped it. (*She leans over the bar to see where it has gone*)
Alfred (*hastily, worried in case she sees he is trouserless*) Don't worry. I'll find it for you.
Mildred I can see it!
Alfred (*in panic*) What?
Mildred No, I can't. It's a bottle-top. What's that thing down there?
Alfred Down where? (*He tries to hide himself behind the tray cloth*)
Mildred It's all right. It's a cork.
Alfred Don't worry about it. I'll find it for you later.
Mildred No, I must find it now. Sentimental value, you understand? (*She slips off the bar stool*) I'll come around and look for it myself.
Alfred No!
Mildred What?
Alfred You can't come round here.
Mildred Why not?
Alfred It's—er—it's indecent.
Mildred It's what?
Alfred It wouldn't be right. I mean, you and me behind the bar—and me without—I mean, me with no . . .
Mildred I'm not going to molest you.
Alfred You wouldn't find it very difficult.
Mildred I wouldn't?
Alfred I mean, I'm a bit vulnerable, if you see what I mean.
Mildred I don't. But I'm willing to find out. (*She makes a move to go behind the bar*)

Alfred Keep back! You can't come round here!
Mildred What's the matter with you?
Alfred I haven't got any trousers on.
Mildred (*after a pause*) You dirty old man!
Alfred Now don't jump to conclusions. There's a perfectly simple—I mean perfectly complicated explanation.
Mildred I'm sure there is.
Alfred And you've got to help me.
Mildred Me?
Alfred Well, you're in trouble too.
Mildred I'm what?
Alfred I mean—you're involved.
Mildred Involved?
Alfred With me. You washed my underpants and that takes a bit of explaining.
Mildred I've never set eyes on your underpants.
Alfred I know. But they think you have.
Mildred Who does?
Alfred Nora and all the rest.
Mildred You're joking.
Alfred Juanito told them.
Mildred Juanito?
Alfred They fell off your balcony.
Mildred Who did?
Alfred My underpants.
Mildred I give up.
Alfred And then of course there's my trousers.
Mildred Your trousers?
Alfred The ones you took to sew a button on.
Mildred They weren't yours.
Alfred They were. So you see you've got to help me.
Mildred How?
Alfred Get me underpants back for a start.
Mildred Where are they?
Alfred In the kitchen. Juanito took them in there.

There is a flash of lightning, followed by a crash of thunder and the sound of rain

Oh hell, here comes the storm! For God's sake hurry up!

Mildred exits through the kitchen arch

Alfred, suddenly realizing he is alone and can make an escape, makes a dash for the dining-room arch. As he reaches it, he realizes someone is coming, so he dives quickly out of sight behind the wicker chair

Rosita enters from the dining-room. Juanito enters up the steps

Juanito Ah, Rosita! Lluve! Mucho! Los cobos! Pronto!

Act II, Scene 1 55

Mildred enters through the kitchen arch with the underpants. She stops short on seeing Juanito and Rosita

Rosita Si! Si! Pronto!

Rosita dashes out through the dining-room arch

Juanito (*to Mildred*) The rain has come, señora. We must make preparations. Excuse me, please.

Juanito dashes off through the kitchen arch

Mildred goes to the bar, looks behind it, and finds that Alfred is missing

Mildred (*looking round*) Mr Tinsley...?
Alfred (*peeping out from behind the chair*) I'm here!
Mildred What are you doing there?
Alfred Hiding.
Mildred Well, here's your underpants. (*She throws them to him*)

Alfred catches the pants. Mildred turns her back on him and he starts to put them on

Nora enters up the steps, and stops short, watching the ensuing scene unnoticed by the other two

You'd better put them on quick before someone sees you.
Alfred They're all stained.
Mildred That's the least of your worries.
Alfred I'll only be half decent with these on. If only you hadn't run off with me trousers.
Nora (*icily*) Don't worry. She'll give them back to you when she's washed them.
Alfred Nora! (*He almost falls over in terror*)

Mildred turns

Nora And I thought you were upstairs in your bed.
Alfred Well, I wasn't.
Nora Then it must've been hers.
Mildred If you think that...
Nora Oh, I don't need to think...
Alfred Now look here, Nora...
Nora I'm doing no more looking. What I see disgusts me. And as for you, Mildred Armitage, you can have him. He's all yours.
Mildred I don't want him.
Nora Oh, I see. Then he's just a passing fancy?
Mildred I never fancied him.
Nora I can imagine that.
Alfred Nora! Stop jumping to conclusions.

Nora Just answer me one question. Where were you when we all went down to the beach?

Water suddenly starts to trickle through the ceiling on to Alfred's head. He moves his position

Alfred It's raining.
Nora I know it's raining.
Alfred Through the bloody ceiling!
Nora Don't try to evade my question. Where were you?
Alfred Behind the bar. And if you don't believe me, ask Ron and Fritz!

Juanito enters from the kitchen arch carrying a number of buckets, which he starts to place in strategic positions to catch the drips of water coming through the ceiling

There is another crash of thunder

Gloria runs in up the steps from the beach, and stops short at the sight of Alfred in his underpants

Gloria What's going on?
Nora What's going on? Plenty! Between your mother and my husband.
Gloria (*incredulously*) You're joking?
Mildred I'll say. When I go for another husband it'll be something less decrepit than him.
Alfred Hey! I thought you said I wasn't a bad sort.
Mildred I did. But that doesn't mean I want you for keeps.
Nora But you don't mind having him on loan.
Mildred Don't talk stupid. If anyone's been having a bit on the side it's your son.
Nora Are you referring to Ron?

Rosita enters from the dining-room, carrying buckets

Mildred Yes, I am referring to Ron. (*Indicating Rosita*) And her!
Nora I don't believe it.
Mildred Then ask her.
Nora Rosita!
Rosita Si, señora?
Nora Have you and my son been er—been having—er . . . ?
Rosita No, no, no, señora! It is Juanito and—(*pointing to Gloria*)—her!
Mildred What?
Gloria It's not true.
Juanito Señora, there is only one girl I wish to marry and that is Rosita.
Rosita Oh! Juanito! (*She drops the buckets, runs to him, and embraces him passionately*)
Alfred (*holding out his arms*) And there's only one woman I want to stay married to, and that's Nora.

Act II, Scene 2

Nora Oh no. That won't wash with me, Alfred Tinsley.

There is another flash of lightning and a crash of thunder

Ron rushes in up the steps, dressed in oilskins

Gloria Ron!

Ron ignores her and rushes across to the telephone above the bar

Ron (*picking up the receiver*) We need the lifeboat. (*He starts to dial*)
Nora What's happened? Where's Grandma?

Grandma enters up the steps, dressed in overlarge oilskins

Grandma I'm here! And I've got me teeth. (*She holds them aloft*)
Ron It's not Grandma, it's Fritz and Elsie! They're in the boat. And it's been swept out to sea!
Juanito Madre mia!

Rosita crosses herself

Alfred I knew it! I knew we should have gone to Blackpool!

A deluge of water descends upon Alfred, as—

the CURTAIN falls

SCENE 2

The same. Early next morning

The storm has abated and the sun is shining again. Juanito is clearing up, emptying ashtrays and cleaning the tables. Alfred and Ron enter up the steps from the beach. Alfred is exhausted, and flops into a chair

Juanito No luck, señors?
Ron Not a sign.
Juanito How far have you been?
Alfred We've searched every bloody beach from here to Scunthorpe. (*He empties sand from his shoes*) My feet are killing me.
Juanito I will make you some coffee.
Alfred Thanks. (*Juanito moves to the kitchen arch*) And throw in a couple of fried eggs, some rashers of bacon, fried bread, mushrooms and tomatoes.
Juanito Si, señor.

Juanito exits through the kitchen arch

Alfred Did he say "yes"?
Ron He did.

Alfred That'll be the first square meal I've had since we got here. It's coming to something when someone's got to drown before you get a decent breakfast.
Ron We don't know yet that they are drowned.
Alfred They'd have turned up by now if they weren't.
Ron I think we ought to go and have another search down by the rocks.
Alfred Relax. You're as fidgety as your mother. She was up and down all night—crying, praying, lighting candles in the window. I hardly got a wink of sleep.
Ron Consider yourself lucky you got any.
Alfred Why?
Ron If I hadn't confirmed that there was nothing between you and that Armitage woman, Mother wouldn't have let you rest at all.

Nora enters from the dining-room, carrying her handbag and dressed completely in black. She walks slowly and tragically

Ron and Alfred gape. Alfred raises his eyes heavenwards

Nora Well—what's the news?
Alfred There isn't any.
Nora No crumb of comfort?
Alfred There will be in five minutes. Juanito's just cooking it.
Nora How can you mention food at a time like this?
Alfred I'm hungry. I've been up since dawn.
Nora So have I. Preparing myself for the worst.
Alfred So I see. No wonder you used half my baggage allowance.
Nora This dress isn't mine. I borrowed it from Juanito's mother. We must be ready to accept that they are lost.
Ron They're not lost yet, Mum, they're only missing.
Nora You found nothing?
Alfred Not a living soul.
Ron Except Mildred Armitage.
Nora Where?
Alfred Out there—in the sea.
Nora Dead, of course!
Alfred No. Searching like us. On one of them pedal boats.
Nora Obviously looking for Fritz.
Ron I reckon she's covered every inch of that bay.
Alfred I'd put my money on her any time in the Tour de France.
Ron We're going out to search again when we've had some breakfast.
Nora I don't think you need bother. We must accept the worst. There are more important things to do before Grandma gets down.
Alfred Such as?
Nora The arrangements.
Alfred What arrangements?
Nora For the funeral.
Ron Mother!

Act II, Scene 2   59

Alfred You're jumping the gun a bit, aren't you?
Nora Someone has to think of these things. All that remains of poor Elsie —when she's found—will have to be transported back to England. I shall send an immediate wire to her headmistress.
Alfred Good idea. Give her plenty of time to get a collection organized.
Nora The school is on holiday.
Alfred So it is.
Nora The first thing you've got to do is ring the Courier.
Alfred Me?
Nora Yes, you. You're the head of the family.
Alfred (*to himself*) I sometimes wonder.
Nora What's that?
Alfred I said he won't take kindly to being woken up at this time of the morning.
Nora (*rummaging in her bag and producing a card*) Here's his number.
Alfred Can't it wait until after breakfast?
Nora No. He might be off early on one of those coach excursions.
Alfred Hang on a bit. I mean Elsie might still turn up . . . on her feet. If that happened I'd look a right Charlie with a funeral all fixed up for her.
Nora The Courier must be warned. I've given you his number . . . so, get on with it.

He goes to the telephone above the bar

Alfred I don't know how to use this thing.
Nora You lift up the receiver and speak into it.
Alfred I know that. I mean, how do you dial?
Nora With your finger. The number's on the card.

Alfred dials laboriously

Alfred It's ringing.

Nora gives him an exasperated look

Alfred (*into the receiver, looking at the card*) Ah! 'Ello! Is that the Pension Don Juan? (*He pronounces it "Jewan"*)
Ron Juan! Don Juan. (*He pronounces it "Hwan"*)
Alfred Eh?
Ron It's pronounced "Don Hwan".
Alfred (*into the receiver*) Don Hwaaan? . . . It is? Ah! Good! Right! (*To the others*) Who do I want?
Nora (*exasperated*) The Courier. Mr Beaverbrook.
Alfred (*into the receiver*) Are you there? (*Pause*) Then slow down a bit.
Nora (*making a move to go to the telephone*) Here—let me do it!
Alfred (*into the receiver*) Hello. I wish to speak to Señor Beaverbrook. (*Pause*) Blooming foreigners yakking away there in Spanish. Can't get any sense out of this bloke. (*Into the receiver*) I want—oh, you *are* Mr Beaverbrook. Well, I'm very glad to hear it. How are you? . . . I'm very well, too . . . What? . . . Oh, my name's Tinsley. Alfred Tinsley . . .

That's right... Sunkissed Tours... We met at the airport two days ago... Remember? Grandma lost her shoe getting off the plane... That's right... Five of us... We're at the Pension Maria in Formentera. (*To the others*) He remembers us. (*Into the receiver*) What? Oh, yes! Yes, they're looking after us very well. Very well indeed... Eh? ... No. No complaints...
Nora Get on with it.
Alfred (*into the receiver*) It's just that... It's about our Elsie... Eh?... She's my sister-in-law. One of the party. Or at least, she was. Or maybe she still is. We don't know yet...
Nora Oh, for heaven's sake! Get to the point. Ask him about the funeral.
Alfred (*into the receiver*) No, it's quite simple really, Mr Beaverbrook. She's passed on... That's right, gone before. At least, that's what our Nora thinks; I'm not so sure. You see, she's missing... Yes, since last night. I know some people do stay out all night when they're on holiday ... What?... Not Elsie. She's not that sort...
Nora I should think not.
Alfred (*into the receiver*) She went off in a boat and hasn't come back yet... I know there was a storm. We got it here too. Inside as well as out... Eh? Holes in the bloody ceiling, that's what. Soaked to the skin, we were... No, I'm not complaining. At least we were able to wash. Made a change to see a drop of water when there's none in the taps...
Nora (*grabbing the receiver*) Oh, come here! (*Into the receiver*) Mr Beaverbrook? This is Mrs Tinsley. My husband's a little overwrought, so perhaps you would talk to me.
Alfred Me, overwrought?
Nora (*into the receiver*) Now, about this terrible tragedy that has befallen my sister—we'd all be grateful if you could advise us on what we should do during this period of anxious uncertainty... I see... The arrangements will, I assume, be provisional?... Oh, I quite agree... money is immaterial at a time like this.

Alfred reacts at the mention of money

Of course, we'll let you know immediately anything transpires... Certainly... Au revoir for now. (*She replaces the receiver*)
Alfred What's all this about money being immaterial?
Nora Mr Beaverbrook was mentioning the cost of the arrangements.
Alfred Oh, he was, was he?
Nora Yes, normally such matters are taken care of by the insurance policy you neglected to take out.
Alfred So?
Nora So put it this way. You've been ten pounds wise and two hundred pounds foolish.
Alfred Two hundred quid?!
Nora That's right.
Alfred Just to get our Elsie back home?
Nora With due reverence.

Act II, Scene 2

Alfred And how much less without the reverence?
Nora Alfred Tinsley! I don't know how you can think of money at a time like this.
Alfred I don't know how I can't think of money at a time like this. We could have brought your Uncle Albert, your Auntie Rose and your cousin Ethel on holiday with us for what it'll cost to get Elsie back.
Nora Don't be so mercenary!
Alfred That settles it—she's got to be found—alive! Come on, Ron. We've got some more searching to do.
Ron What about your breakfast?
Alfred How can you think of food at a time like this?

Grandma enters from the dining-room. She is all merry and bright and dressed in gay clothes and a large colourful sun-hat. They all gape at her

Grandma Morning! What's the matter? Couldn't you sleep?
Nora Mother! Whatever are you thinking of—dressed up like that?
Grandma Never mind me. What are you doing dressed up like that?
Nora I should have thought it was obvious.
Grandma It's not obvious to me.
Nora You've no right to be cheerful at a time like this.
Grandma 'Course I have. I've got me old teeth back.
Nora And at what cost!
Grandma They didn't cost anything. They're National Health.
Nora I'm not talking about money. I leave that to Alfred. (*Dramatically*) All the money in the world couldn't replace what we've lost.
Grandma What do you mean?
Nora You may have found your teeth, but you've lost a daughter.
Grandma Who? Elsie?
Nora Poor little Elsie.
Grandma What's wrong with her?
Nora She's at the bottom of the sea.
Grandma Still looking for sea urchins?
Nora No. Drowned!
Grandma Drowned? Don't talk daft. Our Elsie can't drown. There's not enough of her to sink. When she was a kid she fell in the canal regular as clockwork—and survived!
Nora We've got to face facts. She and Fritz have been missing since last night.
Grandma Have you looked in his bedroom?
Nora Mother!
Alfred I never thought of that.
Ron I'll go and look.

Ron exits through the kitchen arch

Alfred And knock first.

Grandma If I were Elsie I'd prefer that to drowning.
Nora I'd sooner drown.
Alfred So I've noticed.
Grandma You haven't always thought that way, Nora. You and Alfred had your moments...
Nora Mother, please!
Alfred They might have been moments then but they're annual events now.
Nora Alfred! That's enough!
Grandma Anyway, it's about time our Elsie settled down. If Ron finds them up there together I'll make sure they get married. Come to think of it I wouldn't mind having Fritz as a son-in-law. I reckon she could do a lot worse. (*To Nora*) I mean—look what you got!
Alfred Thanks very much!

Mildred enters from the beach dressed in a beach robe. She is somewhat exhausted

Mildred Oh, my legs! My poor legs! I must sit down! (*She staggers to a chair, sits and stretches her legs out. They continue to go through the motions of pedalling*) I've pedalled so much I can't keep them still. I must've been round that bay a dozen times.
Alfred We saw you.
Nora Did you find anything?
Mildred Plenty. I was just turning back when I saw it.
Nora A body?
Mildred No, an island.
Alfred Where?
Mildred Round the headland. It's only small. A few rocks, some reeds and a clump of bushes.
Nora They were on it?
Mildred No, but they'd been there.
Alfred How do you know?
Mildred Something flapping attracted my attention.
Grandma A seagull?
Mildred No. A pair of trousers tied to a boat paddle. The ones I gave Fritz.
Alfred My blooming pants!
Mildred Acting as a distress signal—so they must be safe.
Nora But where are they now?

Ron enters through the kitchen arch

Ron They're not in Fritz's room.
Alfred And they're not on the island. What about the boat?
Mildred No sign of it.
Nora Sunk! I knew it! They're drowned!
Alfred Aw, come off it, Nora. Don't be so morbid. For heaven's sake look on the bright side. There's two hundred quid at stake.

Act II, Scene 2   63

Juanito enters from the kitchen

Juanito Breakfast is ready, señor.
Alfred About time. Come on, let's all go and have something to eat.
Nora I'd choke.
Alfred Don't do that. I don't want to pay another two hundred quid to get you home.
Grandma Come on, Nora. Just a cup of coffee.
Nora Oh, all right.
Mildred I could eat a horse.
Juanito That is for lunch, señora.
Mildred You're kidding?
Juanito No, señora. Very fresh. Straight from the bullring.
Mildred I'll take the fish.
Juanito No fish today, señor. No boat. Please take your places in the dining-room. The breakfast is getting cold.

Grandma, Nora, Mildred and Ron exit to the dining-room

Alfred is about to follow

One moment, please, señor.
Alfred Well.
Juanito My father wishes me to tell you how grieved he is over what has happened . . .
Alfred That's very kind of him. Very kind indeed.
Juanito Yes, the boat has been in the family for a long time.
Alfred The boat?
Juanito For three generations. It is a big loss.
Alfred So it's the boat he's worried about?
Juanito Naturally.
Alfred How much?
Juanito Two hundred and seventy-five thousand pesetas, señor.
Alfred How much in real money?
Juanito Two thousand pounds, señor.
Alfred Hell's bells! We could have ten funerals for that!
Juanito Perhaps you can talk to him later. Your breakfast is getting cold. You will wish to save your bacon.
Alfred It's too blooming late for that!

Alfred exits to the dining-room. Juanito shrugs and follows him off. Fritz enters from the beach. He is dressed in his diving outfit and has obviously just swum ashore. After satisfying himself that there is no-one about he goes to the parapet and calls

Fritz Come. There is no-one about.

Elsie enters. She is dressed in her swimming outfit and has also just swum ashore. She has garlands of flowers round her neck and hibiscus blooms stuck in her hair. She is obviously excited and happy and has fallen for Fritz in a big way

Elsie Oh, Fritzie, you should've carried me over the threshold. (*She goes up to him and winds some convolvulus around his neck*)
Fritz I vill give you a little nip——
Elsie Oh, you are awful!
Fritz —of brandy! To keep out the cold. (*He goes behind the bar*)
Elsie I'm too excited to feel cold. Besides, I never drink alcohol.
Fritz Then now is the time to learn, ja?
Elsie I don't think I should.
Fritz Vell, I do.
Elsie Oh, you're a terrible man. The things you've made me do in such a short time.

Fritz emerges from behind the bar with the drinks and gives one to Elsie

Fritz Cheers!
Elsie Cheers!

They drink

Fritz You are tired after what we did together—ja?
Elsie I'm too elated to be tired.
Fritz It is the first time you have done it?
Elsie Done what?
Fritz Stayed out all night...
Elsie Yes. Except with the Guides.
Fritz You were not afraid?
Elsie Oh, no. Brown Owl always kept an axe handy inside the tent.
Fritz I mean, you were not afraid with me?
Elsie Oh, no. It was so exciting. Just the two of us—lying there—under the stars—the moon shining...
Fritz Ve should have had gypsy fiddlers.
Elsie Or my guitar.
Fritz You suffer from that?
Elsie No, silly. I play it.
Fritz You have hidden talents. There is much of you I have not seen.
Elsie And you're not going to, Fritzie, darling. Not 'til the knot's tied.
Fritz I do not understand.
Elsie You will, after they all hear about last night. You know, this brandy is making me feel quite swimmy.
Fritz Have another.
Elsie I shouldn't. But I will.
Fritz (*refilling her glass*) There.
Elsie Oh, Fritzie, I'm so happy. To have met someone like you.
Fritz I am glad.
Elsie But you know you were very naughty—very naughty indeed.
Fritz I vos?
Elsie Yes. You know what you did?

Act II, Scene 2

Fritz (*worried*) No?
Elsie You leaned over and put your—put your . . .
Fritz (*still worried*) Ja?
Elsie You put your arm round me.
Fritz To keep you warm.
Elsie You were trembling.
Fritz With ze cold.
Elsie That's what you say—you naughty man!
Fritz Elsie, there is something I must tell you.
Elsie (*expectantly*) Yes, Fritzie?
Fritz It is not easy for me to say.
Elsie Don't be bashful.
Fritz Elsie . . .
Elsie Yes?
Fritz I am very glad to have met you.
Elsie (*disappointed*) Oh, so am I. You can give me a kiss.
Fritz Vot?
Elsie A kiss. You know—one of those things where you put your lips together. (*She puckers her lips and makes a kissing sound*)
Fritz I think we should go upstairs.
Elsie Ooh! You are awful!
Fritz To change into our clothes.
Elsie I can't. It's too early. I'd wake Grandma.
Fritz There is my room.
Elsie Ooh! There you go again!
Fritz No, no, I did not mean . . .

The sound of voices drifts in from the dining-room

Wait! (*He goes swiftly to the dining-room arch and peeps in*) Your family. They are in there having breakfast—so you can go to your room and change. But hurry—they'll be out in a minute.
Elsie Just one little kiss before I go.
Fritz All right. Just one.

Elsie closes her eyes and puckers her lips. In desperation Fritz gives her a quick peck on the cheek

(*Propelling her to the kitchen arch*) Now, go quickly. This way . . .
Elsie I won't be long. I can't wait to tell everyone about us.

Elsie exits through the kitchen arch

Fritz starts to move back into the patio, then notices a telegram addressed to him in the letter-rack. He opens it and starts to read

Mildred enters from the dining-room

Mildred Fritz! Oh, Fritz! You're safe!
Fritz (*furtively folding up the telegram*) It depends vot you mean by safe.

Mildred I've been searching for you. Ever since dawn—on a pedal-boat. I thought you were drowned.
Fritz We found an island.
Mildred I know. I found it too. But you'd gone. What happened to the boat?
Fritz It floated away in the night. So we swam ashore.
Mildred Where's Elsie?
Fritz Gone to change.
Mildred You should never have got mixed up with her.
Fritz I am beginning to think so, too.
Mildred If only you'd—well, if only you'd stayed behind with me . . .
Fritz It would have been better perhaps . . .
Mildred I'm sure it would. She's got a terrible reputation with men, you know. She didn't—er—I mean—excuse me for asking—but there were no relations with her, I hope?
Fritz No. They are all having breakfast.
Mildred That's not what I meant. It's just that I was wondering if—whether the two of you—together—all night—on an island . . .
Fritz I did not lay on her . . .
Mildred I should hope not!
Fritz I did not lay on her a finger.
Mildred Oh, Fritz! How gallant of you. You must have had an awful time fighting her off.
Fritz I did. I mean—I just have.
Mildred You should hear the things they say about her at home. Man mad, she is. It's all that biology. Teaching about birds and bees all day puts ideas into her head. But never mind about that. The main thing is you've come back to me.

Gloria enters from the beach, unseen by the other two

Fritz To you?
Mildred But of course. We've still the rest of the holiday together. And then there's the future . . .
Fritz Future?
Mildred Well, I mean we're both of us unattached—and fond of each other—and then there's my little nest egg . . .
Fritz Vot is a nest egg?
Mildred Money in the bank.
Fritz You have money?
Mildred My Sammy wasn't a bookmaker for nothing. So, how about you and me . . . ?
Fritz I must go and change.
Mildred But you haven't answered my question.
Fritz I will tell you when I am dressed.

Mildred kisses him quickly and impulsively

Mildred There! (*Coyly*) There'll be plenty more of those when you've said "yes".

Act II, Scene 2

Fritz exits through the kitchen arch

Mildred turns and sees Gloria

How long have you been there?
Gloria Long enough.
Mildred Fritz and I were just having a little discussion.
Gloria Sounded more like an auction sale.
Mildred Don't be so rude.
Gloria I wonder what his answer'll be?
Mildred "Yes" of course.
Gloria Supposing he finds the money's in trust to me and you only get the interest?
Mildred You wouldn't tell him?
Gloria Why not? You've tried to stop me marrying Ron. Why shouldn't I do the same with you and Fritz?
Mildred Now, listen to me, Gloria. I've only done what I thought was best. Ron's not such a bad lad, I 'spose.
Gloria That's a start anyway.
Mildred And now we know there's nothing between him and that Rosita girl, well, I 'spose I could put up with him as a son-in-law.
Gloria Do you mean it?
Mildred I haven't much choice.

Ron enters from the dining-room

Gloria Well, here he is. You can tell him yourself. (*Pause*) Go on.
Mildred (*gushing*) Ah, Ron, how nice to see you!
Ron But you've just seen me in there.
Mildred How nice to see you again.
Ron Are you feeling all right?
Gloria Of course she is. And you've a confession to make, haven't you, Mum?
Mildred Have I?
Gloria Yes. She wants you to know that she's completely misjudged you in thinking there was something between you and Rosita. Isn't that so, Mum?
Mildred (*after a slight pause*) Yes . . .
Ron She's been drinking.
Mildred Not at this time of the morning.
Ron Then this means you no longer object to Gloria and me getting married?
Mildred I won't stand in her way if she still wants you.
Ron Good God! (*To Gloria*) Did you hear what she said?
Gloria I did.
Ron Then what about it?
Gloria Oh, Ron! (*She runs to him. They embrace and kiss and hold it for quite some time*)

Mildred Don't eat her. You've had your breakfast.
Gloria (*breaking away*) Oh, Ron! I'm so happy.
Ron Me, too! You know, you're not such a bad sort after all, Mrs Armitage.
Mildred Mother.
Ron (*hesitantly*) Mother?
Mildred And you can kiss me.
Ron (*horrified*) Now?
Mildred It's quite usual to kiss one's mother-in-law on these occasions.
Ron Oh? I mean, do I have to? I mean . . .
Mildred (*extending welcoming arms*) Welcome to the family, Ron.

Ron looks around desperately, but realizing there is no escape he goes to Mildred reluctantly. She enfolds him in her arms and kisses him

Alfred, Nora and Grandma enter from the dining-room

Alfred Bloody hell!
Ron We're going to be married!
Alfred You must be off your nut.
Ron Not to her. To Gloria. (*This news is met with silence*) Well, say something.
Nora I think we should get the funeral off our hands before we start thinking of weddings.
Mildred There won't be any funeral. They're both back.
Nora When?
Mildred About twenty minutes ago. They're upstairs getting changed.
Grandma I always knew she was safe.
Alfred (*anxiously*) What about the boat?
Mildred It drifted off into the night. They swam ashore.
Alfred That's two hundred up and two thousand down.
Nora Can't you think of anything else but money?
Alfred It would have been cheaper the other way round.
Nora Alfred Tinsley!

Elsie enters from the kitchen arch. She is radiant, and is dressed very colourfully

Elsie Hello, everyone.
Nora Elsie! (*She embraces Elsie*)
Alfred You've had us all worried stiff.
Nora We thought you were drowned.
Alfred Nora had your funeral cut and dried right down to the ham tea.
Nora Alfred!
Alfred We've just been arguing whether it was to be the Co-op or the Kardoma.
Nora Divi or no divi, I still say the Kardoma.
Grandma Well, you'd better get it settled 'cos it looks like being a wedding breakfast instead.

Act II, Scene 2

Juanito enters through the kitchen arch with Rosita

Elsie Mother, how did you know?
Grandma How did I know what?
Elsie That I was getting married?
Grandma I didn't. I was thinking of Ron.
Elsie Ron's getting married?
Ron That's right. To Gloria.
Elsie But that's wonderful. We'll have a double wedding. Congratulations.
Ron
Gloria } Thanks very much. { (*Speaking together*)
Grandma No need to ask who your intended is. Not after last night's tryout.
Elsie There was nothing like that.
Juanito Who is the lucky man, señorita?
Elsie Herr Grotz.

There is a look from Mildred which says "Oh, no he isn't"

Juanito Then we must make it a big celebration because Rosita and I are getting married too.
Alfred Good for you, Juanito.

There is a chorus of congratulations

Nora Come on, Alfred. Order drinks all round.
Alfred What? With two thousand down on that bloody boat?
Juanito But the boat is found, señor.
Alfred Then why didn't you say so?
Juanito I have only just heard. It was washed ashore—down the coast.
Alfred By God! This does call for a celebration! Bring out the champagne, Juanito.
Juanito Certainly, señor.

Juanito and Rosita start to open two bottles of champagne

Alfred And fill up as many glasses as you can find.

There is a general noise of laughter and gaiety

Mildred (*raising her voice above the noise*) Stop! Stop it at once I say!

There is a sudden silence

Alfred Now, come on, Mildred, don't be a spoil sport. After all, it's your daughter's wedding we're celebrating.
Mildred Then it's up to me to choose where to hold the reception.
Gloria I don't mind the Kardoma, Mum. Or the Co-op for that matter.
Alfred That's my girl.
Mildred Well, I do. And as my wedding happens to be involved as well . . .
Nora Your wedding?
Alfred Don't tell us you're getting spliced as well as our Elsie?

Mildred Not as well as, instead of . . .
Nora What are you talking about?
Mildred Fritz Grotz has proposed to me.
Elsie I don't believe it. He asked me to marry him barely ten minutes ago.
Mildred Then I've beaten you by a short head because he asked me only five minutes ago.
Gloria Mum, that's not quite——
Mildred Shut up, you!
Elsie I can't believe it. It's me he wants to marry—not her.
Mildred You? Who'd want to marry a dried-up old school-marm like you?
Elsie Oooooh!
Mildred All biology theory and no practice.
Elsie And what exactly do you mean by that?
Mildred You should know. He spent all night with you and never touched you.
Elsie Who told you that?
Mildred He did.
Grandma I'm pleased to hear it, Elsie. Don't undo the halter 'til you've got him to the altar.
Elsie Well, he did touch me—so there!
Grandma That settles it, then. (*To Mildred*) Unless he's put a bun in your oven as well?
Mildred Don't be so disgusting.
Grandma Don't you come the old madam wi' me. Everyone in Jubilee Street knows about you and George Skinner. Come to think of it, that bun might be his.
Mildred That's libel!
Grandma No, it isn't—it's slander.
Alfred Ladies, please! There's only one way to settle all this and that's to ask Fritz which one he prefers.
Nora Where is he, anyway?
Mildred Upstairs. Changing.
Alfred If he's got any sense, he'll have scarpered by now . . .

Fritz enters from the dining-room

There is a sudden silence

Elsie (*running to Fritz and tugging at his right arm*) Fritzie!
Mildred (*running to Fritz and tugging at his left arm*) My Fritz!
Elsie Tell them, Fritzie—it's me you're going to marry, isn't it?
Mildred That's absolute rubbish!
Elsie It's not! It's me, isn't it, Fritzie?
Mildred Tell her you proposed to me after you proposed to her.
Elsie But you meant it with me, didn't you? Fritzie, didn't you?
Alfred For heaven's sake shut up, the two of you, and let me get a word in edgeways.

Act II, Scene 2

Pause. Fritz looks first at Mildred, then at Elsie

Do you want me to toss for you? Heads, Elsie—tails Mildred?
Fritz You are both charming and attractive young ladies.

Elsie and Mildred both sigh

Each of you has qualities that any man vould vish for in his bride.

Elsie and Mildred sigh again

I have no hesitation in saying that both of you vill make excellent vives.
Alfred Blimey, he must be a Moslem.
Fritz I vish I vos. There would then be no problem.
Elsie You asked me first.
Mildred Then changed your mind and asked me.
Fritz Ladies, please! I asked neither.
Elsie
Mildred } Yes, you did! { (*Speaking together*)
Fritz I did not. I cannot. And here is the reason ... (*He directs their attention to the steps from the beach*)

Up the steps lumbers Greta, a large German woman generously endowed with flesh. She goes to Fritz with arms outstretched

Greta Fritz!
Fritz I haff received your telegram.
Greta Mein lieben!
Fritz Mein vife!
Alfred Mein God!

Fritz and Greta embrace, to everyone's consternation as—

the CURTAIN *falls*

FURNITURE AND PROPERTY LIST

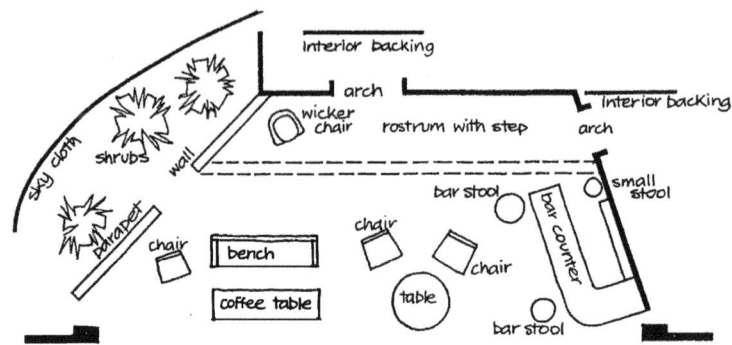

ACT I

Scene 1

On stage: High-backed wicker chair
2 bar-stools
Wooden bench
3 small chairs
Coffee-table. *On it:* ashtray
Occasional table. *On it:* ashtray
Bar. *On it:* ashtray, till, polishing-cloth, tea-cloth, water carafe, ice-bowl and tongs, bottle-openers, packets of nuts, coffee percolator, lemons on plate, fruit-knife, various bottles and glasses. *On shelves inside:* trays, bottle of champagne. *On shelves behind:* orange juice, gin, whisky, rum, brandy, sherry, tonic water, bottles of beer, various bottles of wines and spirits, glasses, cups, saucers, spoons.
On floor: stool
On wall above kitchen arch: letter rack
On wall below kitchen arch: bracket with telephone on long lead

Off stage: Suitcase **(Ron)**
Suitcase **(Alfred)**
2 suitcases **(Juanito)**
Handkerchief **(Gloria)**
Personal: **Alfred:** travel tickets, passports, traveller's cheques, will, postcard, customs form, *Tropical Fish Breeder's Gazette*, pesetas, luggage labels, baggage receipts, gas bill
Fritz: pesetas

Surprise Package   73

                                   SCENE 2
Strike: Dirty glasses
Set: One or two different used glasses on tables and bar
              Wicker chair in original position
Off stage: Tray **(Rosita)**
              Sun-glasses **(Gloria)**
              Bag of chips **(Alfred)**
              Sun-glasses, airbed, inflated water-wings **(Grandma)**
              Beach-bag, goggles, snorkel, fishing-net **(Elsie)**
              Flippers, goggles, snorkel **(Fritz)**
              Tray of bottles and glasses **(Rosita)**
              Net bag of shells and sea urchins **(Fritz)**
Personal: **Ron:** handkerchief

                                   ACT II
                                   SCENE 1
Strike: Broken glass
              Dirty cups, glasses, empty bottles
              Bag of sea urchins
Set: Plate of half-finished food, knife, fork, on bar
              Bottle of beer, bottle of lemonade, glass, on shelf inside bar counter
Off stage: Plate of fish, with knife and fork **(Rosita)**
              Napkin **(Nora)**
              Plate of crême caramel and spoon **(Rosita)**
              Bottle of brandy **(Juanito)**
              Teacloth **(Juanito)**
              Tray with 4 cups of coffee, 4 saucers, 4 spoons, sugar-bowl, cream-jug
                (Rosita)
              Oilskins, sou'westers **(Juanito)**
              Several buckets **(Juanito)**
              False teeth **(Grandma)**
Personal: **Fritz:** pair of tweezers
              Juanito: bottle-opener
              Mildred: cigarettes and lighter in handbag

                                   SCENE 2
Strike: Dishes from bar
              Empty glasses
Set: Telegram in letter-rack under "G"
              2 bottles of champagne behind bar
Off stage: Garlands of flowers and hibiscus blooms **(Elsie)**
Personal: **Nora:** handbag with courier's card

LIGHTING PLOT

Property fittings required: nil
Exterior. A patio. The same scene throughout

ACT I, Scene 1 Day
To open: Effect of brilliant summer sunshine
No cues

ACT I, Scene 2 Day
To open: As previous scene
No cues

ACT II, Scene 1 Day
To open: As previous scene

Cue 1	**Grandma:** "Or go home."	(Page 48)
	Start slow fade to storm effect	
Cue 2	**Alfred:** "Juanito took them in there"	(Page 54)
	Flash of lightning	
Cue 3	**Alfred:** "Ask Ron and Fritz"	(Page 56)
	Flash of lightning	
Cue 4	**Nora:** ". . . wash with me, Alfred Tinsley"	(Page 57)
	Flash of lightning	

ACT II, Scene 2 Day
To open: As opening of previous scene
No cues

EFFECTS PLOT

ACT I

Scene 1

Cue 1	**Juanito:** ". . . señor. I promise you."	(Page 2)
	Ancient taxi draws up	

Scene 2

No cues

ACT II

Scene 1

Cue 2	**Alfred:** "Juanito took them in there"	(Page 54)
	Thunder following lightning flash, then rain. Continue rain, becoming heavy, to end of scene	
Cue 3	**Nora:** ". . . down to the beach?"	(Page 56)
	Water trickles through ceiling	
Cue 4	**Alfred:** ". . . ask Ron and Fritz"	(Page 56)
	Thunder	
Cue 5	**Nora:** ". . . wash with me, Alfred Tinsley"	(Page 57)
	Lightning flash and thunder	
Cue 6	**Alfred:** ". . . gone to Blackpool!"	(Page 57)
	Deluge of water through ceiling	

Scene 2

No cues